LOOK WHAT'S HAPPENED TO PIXIE DE COSTA!

*A Trash Classic in Two
Fast Red Hot Acts*

by

Bruce R. Coleman

LOOK WHAT'S HAPPENED TO PIXIE DE COSTA received its world premier at
Theatre Too! at Theatre Three in Dallas, Texas on October 3, 2008 with the following cast:

Viddy Johnson .... Phyllis Cicero
Young Pixie/Orderly ....Didi Duron
Young Margot/Orderly/Sailor .... Marla Jo Kelly
Pixie De Costa/ Margot De Costa ....Paul Taylor
Henry De Costa/Emory Breedlove/Miss Beezus..............................Ted Wold
Ermangarde De Costa/ Helena La Mancha ....Lisa Ann Haram
Moskovitz/ Eddie Grant..Rick Espaillat
Simpson/ O'Halleran ....Steve Lovett
Newsboy/ Chip Novemberino ....Chad Peterson

Directed by Bruce R. Coleman, with set design by David Walsh, lighting design
by Paul T. Arnold, sound design by Richard Frohlich, and costumes by Bruce R.
Coleman. The Stage Manager was Terry Vandivort, the Assistant Stage Manager was
John Davenport.

*To prevent spoiling THE TRUTH about Pixie/Margot, the actor portraying both roles
was credited in all publicity for the role of "Redd Herring," while Pixie was played
by "Marjorie Keyes" and Margot was played by "Evelyn Rambeaux."*

A NOTE ON STYLE

*Act in the Grand Style of Old Hollywood, before the Method came along and
screwed it all up! Be lush and romantic. Find a sort of Artificial Realism inside the
melodrama. The characters must believe every word they say. To the bottom of their
souls.*

LOOK WHAT'S HAPPENED TO PIXIE DE COSTA!

A Trash Classic in Two Fast Red Hot Acts

by Bruce R. Coleman

*With apologies to Whatever Happened to Baby Jane, Sunset Boulevard, Imitation
of Life, Mildred Pierce, Double Indemnity, A Streetcar Named Desire, The Maltese
Falcon, Kiss Me Deadly, and Lord help us, The Sound of Music.....*

CAST OF CHARACTERS

VIDDY JOHNSON: A Powerful Black Woman. She is the paid companion to the De Costa Sisters. Shoots from the hip and takes no lip. She adores Margot. Pixie? Not so much....Knows THE TRUTH. Narrates from beyond the grave.

YOUNG PIXIE: Age 10. Spoiled, precocious, and used to getting what she wants. Dressed as a Raggedy Ann doll with tap shoes. Part of the De Costa Family's act.

YOUNG MARGOT: Age 12. Quiet, sensitive, used to being in Pixies shadow. Dressed as a Raggedy Ann doll with tap shoes. Part of the De Costa Family's act.

HENRY DE COSTA: The girls' father. He acts as manager for the family's vaudeville act. Dotes on Pixie, Ignores Margot. Dressed in a Straw Hat and Striped Blazer. Part of the act.

ERMANGARDE DE COSTA: The girls' mother. Takes a backseat to Henry when it comes to raising the girls. Has a soft spot for Margot because she understands what it is like to be steam rolled. Dressed in Red and White Striped vaudeville costume with Picture Hat and Parasol. Part of the act.

NEWSBOY: Never changes. Always on the corner, shouting out the news. He is partial narrator along with Viddy.

MOVIE PRODUCER MOSKOVITZ: Big Time producer with a Big Time movie studio, Ready to give Margot the big build up. Ready to show Pixie the door. Wears a Tux.

MOVIE PRODUCER SIMPSON: Small time producer with Big Time movie studio. Glorified Yes man. Ready to agree with whatever Moskovitz wants. Wears a Tux.

PIXIE DE COSTA: Age 54. A drunken Hag has-been. Crude and rough around the edges. As spoiled as an adult as she ever was as a child. Her total lack of feeling and couth is only matched by her total lack of talent. Bette Davis at her worst. Wears clothes that retain a tinge of her former glamour, but are stained with many years worth of bad habits. Believes herself to still be sexually attractive and desirable. She is completely misinformed. Unaware of THE TRUTH.

MARGOT DE COSTA: Age 56. Gracious and glamorous movie star of yesterday. Pixie's sister. As gentle and kind as Pixie is rude. She has been confined to a wheelchair after a horrible…accident ended her career and nearly ended her life. Joan Crawford at her best. Dressed in a classy caftan and Turban, probably designed for her by Schiaparelli many years ago. Unaware of THE TRUTH.

EMORY BREEDLOVE: Flamboyant gay neighbor. An endless encyclopedia of movie trivia and all things fabulous. Cannot believe his good fortune in living next to a Movie Legend. Truly loves and adores Margot De Costa and the forgotten Hollywood she represents. A true Romantic. Wears Lavender and Rose and sports a scarf around his neck. Unaware of THE TRUTH.

MISS BEEZUS: Emory's Persian cat. Obviously phony, but played as real. Emory supplies Miss Beezus' meows and purrs.

HELENA LA MANCHA: Gossip columnist with the L. A. Times Record. A doppelganger for Louella Parsons. Genteel and cultured on the radio, where she holds forth on her daily Hollywood gossip program; Bossy, Bitchy and crass in real life. Not above using everything in her power to land a story. Has been waiting for YEARS for a crack to appear in the De Costa sisters' façade. Wears a floral hat and Dior's New Look just like her god, Hedda Hopper. Pure Evil. Knows THE TRUTH.

EDDIE GRANT: Out of work screenwriter. Tough as nails former dope addict. Think Bogey, Cagney and John Garfield rolled into one, and then run him over with a city bus. Wears crummy suit and crummy tie. Unaware of THE TRUTH.

CHIP NOVEMBERINO: Sweet innocent hunky electrician. Early twenties. He is here to help his father out and fix a faulty wall socket in the De Costa's apartment. Classically Hollywood gorgeous, but unaware of his appeal. Wears a wife-beater tee shirt and dungarees, with a tool belt slung around his heavenly hips... Needs to look good naked (or nearly) when he strips down to his jockey shorts. This is NOT his lucky day. Unaware of THE TRUTH.

INSPECTOR O'HALLERAN: Typical Irish Cop. Steady in his temperament, but we must sense danger lurking underneath. Wears a beat up suit and trench coat, with a slouchy hat pulled over his head. Knows THE TRUTH.

HOSPITAL ORDERLIES: Two ladies in uniform, capes, and white hose with really long needles full of muscle relaxers.

Act I

(A swirling void emanates from center stage. Purple. Green. It Sparkles. The eerie science fiction strains of the Theremin creep slowly in, humming and purring. Suddenly, a newsboy darts out from the morass, plying his trade.)

NEWSBOY: EXTRA EXTRA! Read all about it! De Costa Sisters Scandal Rocks Hollywood! Home town of Virtue and Decency Embroiled in HOT NEW Murder Case! Old wounds pried open with rusty screwdriver! Extra Extra!

(A golden shaft of light suddenly cuts through the whirlpool of sound and color, illuminating a figure. The figure of a powerful black woman. She is dressed and coiffed not unlike Miss Juanita Moore in 'Imitation of Life' The figure stands straight and tall, arms reaching toward us like a Val Lewton Zombie. She is a Voodoo Priestess. She is a keeper of THE TRUTH. She has every other Wednesday off. She speaks from beyond the grave.)

VIDDY: Hold on there a minute, boy!

NEWSBOY: Paper lady?

VIDDY: Yes! I'll take a paper.

NEWSBOY: That'll be two bits.

VIDDY: Here you go....

NEWSBOY: Thanks!

VIDDY: That's quite a picture they got splashed across the front page.

NEWSBOY: Yeah! Ain't that somethin'? Look at all them stiffs! Must have been some massacre! Reminds me of what's left over after a Capone-style gangland hit. Who would believe that all that took place in a high price, high and mighty, high rise apartment...?

VIDDY: Me, for one! Because that's exactly where it did take place. Way up there on the fourteenth floor of the Hollywood Ritz Arms Hotel.

NEWSBOY: Oh yeah? How do you know so much?

VIDDY: I was there.

NEWSBOY: You a witness?

VIDDY: No. A victim.

NEWSBOY: WHAT???

VIDDY: Take a look at that picture! That's me, right there!

NEWSBOY: Who you kiddin', lady? The paper says there were no survivors!

VIDDY: Who said I survived? Look at that picture again! Anyone's face ringin' a bell!

NEWSBOY: What the—It IS you!

VIDDY: That's right baby, I am Miss Viddy Johnson and lord help me, I am speaking to you from beyond the grave! And I'd say I look pretty good too, for a woman who spent the night wearing nothing but a toe tag in the city morgue.

NEWSBOY: Holy crap. Hey! Does this make you a ghost? Or one of them flesh eatin' zombies?

VIDDY: No honey. This makes me the NARRATOR! And, the only eyewitness to the horrible events that transpired up there in that dark and musty penthouse… *(Distracted by photo in paper.)* Lord! Just look at this picture! Mm mm mm! Hand to Jesus, would it have killed one of them lazy reporters to have taken three seconds to straighten me up a little bit since I was having my picture took? See there? Got my skirt and petticoats bunched up so far underneath me, you can see all the way up to God's creation! Good thing I had on my nice drawers.

NEWSBOY: Lady, I'd say you got bigger problems than that!

VIDDY: You mean like having a ten pound claw hammer lodged in my skull?

NEWSBOY: Yeah, we could start there.......

VIDDY: Maybe you're right.

NEWSBOY: Jumpin' Jehosaphat! This sure is somethin'! Talkin' to a real live dead person! This kinda stuff NEVER happens to me!

VIDDY: I should hope not!

NEWSBOY: And my guess is that this is kinda new for you too, huh?

VIDDY: Honey, I've been dead right, dead tired, and dead drunk , but I ain't NEVER been just DEAD before! Child, the thing is, I was wrong! I shoulda seen it comin'....I guess I always knew that it just might end up this way. You see I was the paid companion to....no. I don't wanna burden you with my troubles. It's a long story.

NEWSBOY: How long?

VIDDY: I'd say about two hours with intermission.

NEWSBOY: Well, I guess you better get started!

VIDDY: Fair enough. Let me ask you. Who's your favorite movie star?

NEWSBOY: That's easy! Roy Rogers!

VIDDY: And who was it three years ago?

NEWSBOY: I—uh. I—don't remember.

VIDDY: And that's the way it is! There is an old saying in Hollywood. That you are only as good as your last picture. With a hit you're on top— with a miss you go flop. And once you go flop you'll never see top again! Lord help me but its true. But a flop isn't always a bad picture. It can also be a bad break. Or bad luck. That's the way it was for the De Costa sisters.

NEWSBOY: Hey! Yeah! Who are these broads? I never heard of 'em!

VIDDY: Never heard of 'em? Pixie and Margot De Costa. They were big once. Until tragedy cut their reign in Hollywood short. Some folks say that Pixie was dried up—finished—on her way out. Too much booze and too many men. And Margot? Margot's star was on the rise. There wasn't anything she couldn't do. Except keep that one terrible, terrible accident from ending it all....

NEWSBOY: Aw, you lost me!

VIDDY: Then you're gonna have to see it for yourself. Just so you can experience the tragedy first hand! Let me take you back now...back!...BACK!! To a time and place fading into distant memory....a place that looked a lot like the beginning of... THE END!

NEWSBOY: Can you do that?

VIDDY: Sure! Just sit tight and I'll put the hooba jooba on ya!

NEWSBOY: Holy Crap!

(Viddy waves her arms over the Newsboy, who goes into a trance The Music goes wildly out of control as we are hurled backward in time and space. Viddy snaps her fingers and we are transported to 1912. The Newsboy awakens and delivers the head line of the day.)

NEWSBOY: Extra! Extra! World's fair of 1912 opens today! Indonesian Pagoda serves exotic Chicken dishes! Steam powered automatic dishwasher excites the fairer sex!! De Costa Sisters entertain Heads of State! Read All About It!

(He and Viddy sit on the side of the stage and watch the action.. Just then, Henry and Ermangarde De Costa and their adorable little daughters Pixie and Margot enter. They are dressed as turn of the century vaudeville entertainers. The girls are dressed to look like gingham rag dolls. They are standing in front of an olio curtain exclaiming the wonders of the 1912 Worlds Fair. There is a panel that features the De Costa Family and their Act.)

HENRY: Come on, Pixie honey! We can't quit now! You gotta do the act one more time today!

YOUNG PIXIE: No, Daddy! No!

HENRY: Aw, Pixie! Where's my little trouper? Where's daddy's little ray of sunshine?

YOUNG PIXIE: I'm hungry! I hate this dress! AND I'M TOO TIRED!!!

HENRY: Just one more itty bitty song and dance? Just to make your daddy smile?

YOUNG PIXIE: I DON'T WANNA!!

HENRY: Pixie sugar, this is a very important performance! It could mean BIG, BIG things for the De Costa family!

YOUNG PIXIE: Too bad, so very sad! The act doesn't go on unless I say so! And I don't wanna sing and dance right now! I wanna ice cream instead!

ERMANGARDE: Henry, it has been an awfully long day. The girls are exhausted! Perhaps we could forgo a performance just this once and have a little refreshment? Why, there is a frozen custard pavilion right around the corner.

HENRY: Are you out of your mind??? This will be the biggest break we could ever have asked for! Do you know who is out there in the audience tonight? None other than Merriam J. Cantwell!

ERMANGARDE: Who dear?

HENRY: Cantwell! CANTWELL!! What is the matter with you! Merriam J. Cantwell is only the biggest producer of Nickelodeons and Movin' Pictures in the whole country!

ERMANGARDE: I don't see what…

HENRY: No of course ya don't, Ermangarde! Ya don't see…ya don't hear….YA DON'T THINK! That man could mean salvation for this family! One look at what our little Pixie has to offer and he'll fall in love with us! Our shining star will get a contract with his studio, and we'll be out there in Californy livin' like them Pooh-Bahs on EASY street!!

7

ERMANGARDE: Well, if he just needs to see the family perform, lets do the number that features our Margot so little Pixie rest!

YOUNG MARGOT: Oh no! I couldn't!

HENRY: Margot? Bleeeeeeagh! You KNOW Pixie's the one with all the looks and talent! We send Margot out there, its back to the meat packin' warehouse for yours truly! And everybody laughin' at me all over again! Is that what you want?

ERMANGARDE: But Margot....

HENRY: Enough with that! *(Turns to Pixie.)* Look Pixie, ya gotta do this for daddy, alright honey? Everybody I ever knew is just waiting for me to fall on my face. Nothin' ever worked out for me. Stale job. Boring wife. Boring life. Then God blessed me with a child! Well, she didn't work out so hot either, so God blessed me with a second child! You! My little angel. My little package from Heaven! So, Pixie, I'm countin' on you. You gotta prove to the world that your daddy isn't just some big joke! If we go to Hollywood you'll get everything you ever wanted. No dream can be too big!

YOUNG PIXIE: Really, Daddy?

HENRY: Anything you could ask for will be yours!

YOUNG PIXIE: Can I have a pony?

HENRY: You can have twelve!

YOUNG PIXIE: How about a new dress?

HENRY: As many as you could wish for!

YOUNG PIXIE: A new dolly???

HENRY: Yes! Yes! Yes!

YOUNG PIXIE: Oh all right. Just for you. And me, so I can get all the pretty things that I deserve. *(To Margot, sweetly.)* You would deserve them to, Margot!

YOUNG MARGOT: *(Hopefully.)* Yes, Pixie?

YOUNG PIXIE: *(Still sweetly.)* If you was pretty and talented and didn't reek of failure…

YOUNG MARGOT: *(Defeated—again…)* Yes, Pixie.

YOUNG PIXIE: Here I go, daddy! And, Margot. Try to do the steps RIGHT this time. When you mess up, it makes ME look wrong!

YOUNG MARGOT: I'll try Pixie.

YOUNG PIXIE: Now, Lets go make all my dreams come true!

YOUNG MARGOT: *(Meekly.)* I have dreams too!

HENRY: Go Pixie! Go!

ERMANGARDE: And Margot!

HENRY: Yeah. Whatever.

(Henry and Pixie move off to the side.)

ERMANGARDE: Margot darling.

YOUNG MARGOT: Yes Mother?

ERMANGARDE: *(Gently.)* try not to mind your Father and Pixie too much. Especially Pixie. She's not like other little girls! She's …well….strange, exotic and unusual….Yes. Strange. Very strange. Very, very strange….

YOUNG MARGOT: All right mother.

ERMANGARDE: And Margot. You and I both know that you're just as wonderful and talented as your sister. We must remember that, even if THEY don't……

YOUNG MARGOT: I'll remember mother. *(Murderously.)* In fact, I'm never gonna forget any of this…..

(The family prepares to perform.)

HENRY: And Now, Ladies and Gents! Those Adorable Tykes….Those Titanic Tots…..Those Itty Bitty Girls with Lotsa Shiny Curls…..The De Costa Sisters in " The Hi-Larious Hi Jinx of Millie and Tillie, The Dancing Dollies!!"

(Pixie and Margot Launch into their act.)

YOUNG PIXIE: My best friend is Millie!

YOUNG MARGOT: My best friend is Tillie!

YOUNG PIXIE: And you may think its silly

BOTH: But its Twoo!

HENRY: GO, PIXIE, GO!

YOUNG PIXIE: SHUT UP DADDY!

YOUNG PIXIE: But When I said to Millie!

YOUNG MARGOT: That's right! You said so Tillie!

YOUNG PIXIE: Lets go run Willie Nillie

BOTH: Wouldn't You?

HENRY: SPARKLE, PIXIE, SPARKLE!

YOUNG PIXIE: I'M SPARKLING!

YOUNG PIXIE: I never had a better sis than my dear Pal!

YOUNG MARGOT: And there's not been a better miss than this here Gal!

YOUNG PIXIE: And when we go out Millie!

YOUNG MARGOT: We'll watch each Joe pout Tillie!

BOTH: Cause there is no doubt really

BOTH: I'm for you!

(Dance break. The girls tap like the survival of Western Civilization depends upon it!)

YOUNG PIXIE: And when we go out Millie!

YOUNG MARGOT: We'll watch each Joe pout Tillie!

BOTH: Cause there is no doubt really!

BOTH: I'm For…Yooooooooooou!!

(Thunderous applause.)

YOUNG PIXIE: Now where's my pony daddy?

(As the rest of the family exits, Little Margot steps into a light and tears the Millie wig from her head then violently smears her red lipstick viciously across her face, anger seething in her eyes…)

YOUNG MARGOT: Just you wait, Miss Pixie De Costa!

(The olio curtain rolls up and disappears as Viddy reenters.)

VIDDY: Legend has it that the De Costa girls were on fire that day. Before they knew it, they found themselves in Tinsel Town, both of them making movies and tons of geetus.

NEWSBOY: Margot too?

VIDDY: It's a funny thing, but as the years raced by things changed. Pixie may have come out here the headliner, but it was Margot that became the star!

NEWSBOY: No kiddin'?

VIDDY: As those girls grew up Margot's career blossomed! But Pixie? Pixie sunk like the Lusitania! When that happened, Pixie became all eaten up with jealousy. She started drinkin' and carousin' round the clock! While Margot was being wined and dined at the Brown Derby and the Mocambo, Pixie was paying weekly visits to the free clinic. Then one night in 1932 something tragic would happen that would change the course of history. It started in the brand new penthouse apartment that Pixie and Margot shared at the Hollywood Ritz Arms Hotel. And it would end on the pavement 14 stories below....

(1932—The Glamorous interior of the De Costa's Sunset Boulevard Penthouse Apartment at the Hollywood Ritz Arms. It is decorated in the style of Conde Nast and Van Nest Polglase. Upstage there is an entry hallway that we can see through the arched doorway up center. The hallway stage right leads off to the front door, which we do not see. Stage left leads to the kitchen which we also do not see. Inside the living room there are doors stage right. One is a closet and the others are a set of French doors that lead out to the Balcony. Stage Left there is a door leading to Margots bedroom. Down Left is a television set (hidden until we arrive in 1957) and down right there is a desk with a lamp on it. Stage center is a large satin covered Chaise Lounge. The walls are studded with framed pictures of the sisters and framed posters from their movies. It is a monument to De Costa mania! A party is in full swing celebrating the opening of Margot's latest picture! Two Producers, Moskovitz and Simpson enter. They are in tuxedos and carry champagne glasses.)

SIMPSON: Hi-ya, Mr. Moskovitz!

MOSKOVITZ: Good evening, Simpson. Glad you could make it.

SIMPSON: Get a load of this joint! Hoity toity!

MOSKOVITZ: Yes indeed! This is the most exclusive Penthouse apartment on Sunset Boulevard! Why it makes Pickfair look like the county dump...

SIMPSON: Saaaaay, this is quite a swah-ree those De Costa sisters are throwin' here!

MOSKOVITZ: Why not? Margot De Costa's latest picture opened tonight and she's already boffo at the box office. Lines of movie goers circling the block three or four times! People fighting to get a ticket! Why it's a riot! And with the take still rollin' in from her last seven star vehicles, she's ready to take her place as REAL Hollywood royalty!

SIMPSON: And did you see them reviews? Winchell even said that Margot out-Garboed GARBO!

MOSKOVITZ: I tell ya, Simpson. This De Costa girl is a sensation! Why, she'll be a star for years to come!

SIMPSON: Yeah. Too bad the same can't be said about her sister. I suppose Pixie's hangin' around here somewhere, stinko as usual....

MOSKOVITZ: Please! Do not MENTION the name of Pixie De Costa to me! My blood pressure will go through the roof! The bloom on that rose has been replaced with run-a-day gin blossoms. And her 'acting', if you can call it that, is enough to clear the Vatican on Easter Sunday!!

SIMPSON: That lousy, huh?

MOSKOVITZ: Lousy? Her last three pictures stunk up the screen so bad they ended up costing the studio thousands of dollars! You couldn't pay BLIND people to go see 'em. But Margot! Margot! Why, she's electrifying! We just need to get her booze hound sister out of the way.... once and for all.....

SIMPSON: Good thing Pixies contract is up this month.

 MOSKOVITZ: Yes we'll be able to give Pixie the air soon enough! When we get through with that little skeeve, no body will remember that Margot even HAD a sister, let alone the biggest whore-lush in Tinsel Town!

SIMPSON: You are right, boss!

MOSKOVITZ: Say, what is all that commotion out on the balcony.

SIMPSON: Wouldn't ya know it? It's them De Costa sisters! Margot's hot after Pixie for drinkin' all the booze! Say, you don't suppose that Pixie got wind that she was about to receive the heave!

MOSKOVITZ: Ah, who cares? I say good riddance to cheap trash!

SIMPSON: Jeez, I never saw Margot so mad! Hey!

MOSKOVITZ: Hey! Look out there!

SIMPSON: Hey boss! They're getting' awfully close to the railing.

MOSKOVITZ: Pixie! Unhand your sister!

SIMPSON: Boss! The Railing! Its giving way!

MOSKOVITZ: Stop! Stop! Noooooooo!

(Blood-curdling scream from offstage.)

SIMPSON: Oh dear God! She Fell! She Fell!

MOSKOVITZ: She didn't Fall! SHE WAS PUSHED!

SIMPSON: Whatta we gonna do?

MOSKOVITZ: Control yourself Simpson! Get me the phone! I've got a studio to save!

(Viddy reappears.)

NEWSBOY: Holy Cow! What a tough break! Just when things was goin' so good for Margot!

VIDDY: People aren't too clear about what happened next. But one thing was sure. The De Costa sisters practically disappeared over night! No more Movies, no more Premieres, no more parties, No more Margot, No more Pixie.

NEWSBOY: Yeah, but there's more to this story than two washed up movie stars goin' up in a puff of smoke! What gives?

VIDDY: People gossiped about it for years! But like any good parent, the studio stepped in and made everything all better. They swept the hurt under the rug of silence. And they sentenced the memory of the De Costa sisters to imprisonment on the 14th floor of the Hollywood Ritz Arms Hotel.

NEWSBOY: Aw, come on, lady! Spill! How did you wind up as the bottom pancake of a dead body short stack? You gotta tell me what went on up there!

VIDDY: What went on was 25 years of secrets and lies leading up to......yesterday! You see, there was nothing particularly special about how it all started. As paid companion, I came to the penthouse during the week to manage the housework, cook, and keep company. I was up there, preparing to do my chores for the day. A day that would begin with our own Miss Margot De Costa, confined to a wheelchair, watching one of her old movies on television, a tear of nostalgia trickling down her cheek. And Honey, This would NOT be the last tear she would shed before all was said and done.............

(Viddy and Newsboy exit.)

(Lights up on the De Costa Penthouse, today. If today were 1957. Margot, now in her mid fifties sits in a wheelchair and stares intently at a small portable television in front of her. She is a handsome woman, enveloped in a tasteful caftan with a turban wrapped around her head. She is wearing make up that might have been in style in the 1930s. She is a warm, gracious and glamorous presence. She knows that a Star must act like a Star, no matter the circumstance. She is Joan Crawford and Loretta Young at their best.)

VOICEOVER: ...Thank you for including Station KBDS in your television viewing schedule. This is your Morning Movie Spectacular, brought to you by Lux Detergent and General Foods Cereal. We now return to Margot de Costa and Robert Taylor in ' The Duchess and The Other Duchess'.....

(Margot speaks along with her image on the screen.)

MARGOT: Dearest, Darling Sebastian. I do love you. With every breath I take, with every fiber of my being. But my heart, Sebastian. My foolish foolish heart. It knows that I can never possess you. For you belong to another. Dear, plain, Rosamund. Such a simple, simple, …simple girl. Rosamund holds the key to your heart Sebastian, not I. And so I must say…adieu…

(Viddy enters. It is yesterday, so she is alive…for now…)

VIDDY: Miss Margot?

MARGOT: Yes Viddy?

VIDDY: I'm sorry. I thought I heard voices…

MARGOT: It was only me, Viddy darling. Me and the flickering image of my former self.

VIDDY: You were so beautiful in this picture Miss Margot. So full of vitality. So fresh.

MARGOT: Whatever happened to her Viddy? That girl.

VIDDY: I just love when the Morning Spectacular runs your movies Miss Margot. Whether they're showing 'Executive Secretary' or 'I Lived With Evil' or my personal favorite, 'Saint Teresa and the Lepers' I just gotta stop what I am doin', sit myself down and watch. Miss Margot? Are you cryin'?

MARGOT: My darling Viddy. You have been such a good companion to me all these years. I honestly don't think I could have made it through the dark times without your kindness.

VIDDY: Now, don't you go on like that, Miss Margot. Anybody else would have done the very same thing.

MARGOT: No Viddy, I don't think so. So many of the people that I held most dear deserted me after …the accident. I guess they just couldn't bear to see their little gadfly earthbound. But not you, Viddy. You have been my truest friend.

VIDDY: And I always will be Miss Margot.

MARGOT: *(Staring at the television.)* Look at her Viddy. Look at her sparkling eyes and that carefree smile...Forgive a foolish old woman, Viddy. I must always remember that the past is an awfully nice place to visit, but one shouldn't try to live there. Like Encino.

VIDDY: You have every right to feel a little blue sometimes Miss Margot. Not many people have been through what you have. Not many could have survived.

MARGOT: Yes Viddy, I have had my trials. *(Not unkindly.)* Those of us blessed with remarkable gifts do bear a heavier load than those of more common experience. *(The women nod in agreement.)* But, we must remember the glories of life! All those first read-throughs of the script on the set, all those Red Carpet openings, the laughter of small children....

VIDDY: Yes, yes, Miss Margot. Your life has been full of meaning. And sometimes even purpose.

MARGOT: Darling Viddy...

VIDDY: Shall I open the French doors for you? And let in some fresh air?

MARGOT: *(Suddenly a bit jumpy)* Not the French doors! I'm too near the balcony...

VIDDY: It still upsets you doesn't it? Even after all these years?

MARGOT: I am sorry. It does haunt me still. Every moment I spend in this chair is a gruesome reminder of what my life could have been. The shadow of a life never lived passes before my soul like so much torn and burnt celluloid. *(Brightens.)* But, we mustn't allow ourselves to be bitter! For bitterness creates those dreary small lines across the forehead and around the mouth!

VIDDY: Yes ma'am.

MARGOT: Viddy, lets be brave! We'll just go right ahead and open those naughty wittle fwench doors!

VIDDY: Yes ma'am!

MARGOT: Good heavens! Look at the time! It's nearly eleven! We'll be having lunch soon and I haven't heard a peep coming from Pixies room…

VIDDY: No ma'am. I don't expect her to be up for quite awhile.

MARGOT: Oh dear. It's the alcohol isn't it? Viddy you can be honest with me. Pixie has been drinking again, hasn't she?

VIDDY: I try to stop the deliveries from the liquor stores Miss Margot, but she always figures out some kind of new angle to get all of that disgusting hooch up in here. And I tell you something, Miss Margot, dealin' with Miss Pixie sober is one thing, but dealin' with her drunk is another. It's enough to make me take the good Lords name in vain!

MARGOT: I know dear. Pixie can be a trial. But we must show her as much kindness as we can. In some ways, …the accident was harder on her than it was on me. Just knowing that she was responsible for the fall that put me in this chair shattered something in her that no doctor or priest has ever been able to mend. My injuries are superficial. Her scars go much deeper, I am afraid. I lost the use of the lower two thirds of my body that day. But something within Pixie actually died.

VIDDY: Well, I will make a pledge to you, Miss Margot. As God is my witness I will stick by you and we WILL get through all of this just fine!

MARGOT: Viddy, you are a blessing to me. Somewhere in my youth or childhood, I must have done something good.

(Doorbell.)

MARGOT: What on earth?

VIDDY: Ooh, I'll bet you that it's that sweet Mister Emory from across the hall comin' for his visit.

MARGOT: Darling Emory.

VIDDY: Oh honey, that man can make me laugh!

MARGOT: Well show him in!

(Emory enters carrying his cat, Miss Beezus. He is the personification of old school camp. He is dressed in lavender and wears a scarf around his neck. He is REAAAAAALY gay.)

EMORY: Hello everyone! I'm Loretta Young!

MARGOT: Emory! How lovely!

(Miss Beezus, an obviously phony Persian cat that Emory animates as of it were real, shakes and meows…)

EMORY: There, there, Miss Beezus! We must behave ourselves! We have come to see the two most beautiful women on the fourteenth floor of the Hollywood Ritz Arms Hotel!

VIDDY: Now, you go on and stop that Mr. Emory!

EMORY: Why Miss Vivian Johnson! I believe you've gone all weak in the knees like a catholic schoolgirl!

VIDDY: Mr. Emory! Have you had any lunch yet?

EMORY: Darling, eating does not sit at all well with my girlish figure these days!

MARGOT: Oh, Emory, you must have a little something.

EMORY: Alright! Twist my arm! Viddy, I'll have a cucumber sandwich and a cup of hot water! The silhouette this season is pleated pants and I shan't be caught dead looking too hippy!

MARGOT: Viddy, Could you serve us in here?

VIDDY: Yes ma'am. *(She starts to leave.)* It won't take me two shakes of a lamb's tail...

EMORY: Wait Viddy!

VIDDY: What is it Mister Emory?

EMORY: You must come back and leave again so I can watch you shake your OWN tail!

VIDDY: Oooooooh Mr. Emory!

EMORY: Darling Viddy....

MARGOT: Dearest Emory. You are much too much!

EMORY: Or am I never quite enough? *(Sees the television.)* Well, my goodness! Margot De Costa...

MARGOT: Oh yes. This morning they were showing...

EMORY: No, no! No need to tell me. Margot De Costa and Robert Taylor in 'The Duchess and The Other Duchess' I have seen it exactly 37 times. You've just ended it with Sebastian, and as he races back to the arms of his beloved Rosamund, you have climbed the Himalayas with Pepe, your Sherpa, and you are about to throw yourself into the great Ganga-Bramhaputra river basin. Gowns by Adrienne.

MARGOT: And my first Oscar nomination.

EMORY: Your first highway robbery! Just who the HELL was that Louise Rainier schtupping?

MARGOT: Emory! Such language! And it was Irving Thalberg! Drove Norma Shearer CRAZY!

EMORY: Or at least cross eyed!

MARGOT: When I finally did win the statuette, for 'Leave 'em Loving!', it truly was a bitter sweet victory...But, I should feel grateful. Not everyone has this lovely award. Poor Susan Hayward...

EMORY: May I look at it more closely Miss Margot?

MARGOT: Of course dear! Only don't use that lamp. There is a faulty socket that gave Viddy quite a shock the other day. I believe the super is coming later to fix it. Just hold it up to the light from the window.

EMORY: Ah, Miss Margot. I adore watching your films on the Zenith. It reminds me of a time when there really was such a thing as magic. A time when glamour was a religion, and WE were its disciples. A time when beauty was reason enough to hang a story on celluloid. I miss those days. Look! There it is! That beautiful script announcing 'The End' And it really sort of was, wasn't it? The end of glamour and beauty.

MARGOT: As long as we have these sparkling images, Emory, we'll always possess those things.

EMORY: May I make a teensy weensy confession, Miss Margot?

MARGOT: Emory you can tell me anything!

EMORY: I have a very vivid memory of seeing you in this very picture when I was younger. You so transfixed and transported me that I actually....oh its too silly....

MARGOT: Please go on.

EMORY: Well, I actually felt like I became you! For one brief moment. I lived the dream that you were creating! I had become the glory that was Margot De Costa.

MARGOT: Emory that has to be the sweetest compliment I have ever received.

(They share a tender moment together. Then...)

EMORY: Oh, be honest Miss Margot, what was Robert Taylor really like?

MARGOT: To tell you the truth Emory, he was a little stiff....

EMORY: Not according to Barbra Stanwyck!

MARGOT: Oh Emory! The things you say!

(Emery suddenly shakes Miss Beezus and makes the mewing sound.)

MARGOT: Oh dear! Miss Beezus certainly has gotten riled up over something!

EMORY: Ignore her! Ignore her! Miss Beezus just cannot stand it when every eye in the room is NOT focused squarely on her! She is as jealous as Lupe Velez. Isn't that so, Miss Beezus?

(Emory makes wild mewing sounds.)

EMORY: Miss Beezus! I swear I will put you in the basket in the corner if you don't settle down!

(More wild mewing.)

EMORY: All right, little miss! NO cream for you AT ALL tonight!

(The mewing calms down and becomes a purring.)

EMORY: There! I knew that would do it! Miss Beezus cannot exist with out her Carnations! She'll behave now.

MARGOT: I must say Darling Emory, you have the best trained pussy in all of Los Angeles.

EMORY: I thought that was Yvonne De Carlo?

MARGOT: Emory! You are wicked! Why some woman hasn't snatched you up is beyond imagination!

EMORY: Quell Mystere!

MARGOT: I guess I'll just have to count you a member of that elite Hollywood bachelors club that drives us girls MAD: Darling Clifton Webb, That adorable Liberace, Caesar "Butch" Romero, and that gloriously beautiful Mr. Rock Hudson.

EMORY: One can only hope there's a steam room at that club!

MARGOT: Oh Emory! *(Confused.)* What?

EMORY: Speaking of alley cats gone wrong, where is that SISTER of yours this morning?

MARGOT: Still tucked in I'm afraid. She must not be feeling well. Bit of a headache I suppose.

EMORY: Hmmmm. I guess doing the Tango all night with Johnny Walker Red will have that effect…

MARGOT: Emory! What are you saying?

EMORY: Nothing darling.…

MARGOT: Now Emory! I have truly treasured getting to know you and watching our relationship burst forth from the tender buds of friendship. So I insist you not keep things from me.

EMORY: But your health, dear Margot.

MARGOT: Just because I am confined to this chair for the rest of my life with no hope of walking again doesn't mean that I am not strong as an ox! Now please, what is it?

(Emory takes a deep breath and begins his tale of horror!)

EMORY: Miss Margot, you know that outside of Merle Oberon, I think you are the greatest talent the screen has ever known. And you know I would never say anything in the WORLD that might upset you. But what I am about to tell you is indeed SHOCKING and HORRIFYING! Last night at midnight....MIDNIGHT mind you, I was aroused from my slumber by a cacophony that would have wakened the dead! Miss Beezus, bless her, was clawing at the drapes in my boudoir. She was slashing them to ribbons, blood spurting from her nails!

MARGOT: My heavens!

EMORY: I arose from my bed *(for effect)*...nude...and flew to the window like Botticelli's Venus! I gathered Miss Beezus into my arms...nude...to try and comfort her! As we both teetered on the very edge of hysteria, I had no choice but to slap Miss Beezus! I slapped her again and again! And again and again! Calm Down Miss Beezus!, I cried, tears of passion running down my cheeks! At long last, Miss Beezus threw herself against my shoulder and wept like a Cornish milkmaid. I sang to her... .a Schubert art song I think....until she finally succumbed...

MARGOT: Good Heavens! What could have prompted this outburst from her?

EMORY: WELL! It was at that moment that I looked out the window and saw the cause of Miss Beezus's madness. It was your sister, Miss Margot. It was .....PIXIE DE COSTA!

MARGOT: NO!

EMORY: YES!

MARGOT: NO!

EMORY: YES!

MARGOT: That's insane! You must have been mistaken!!

EMORY: It WAS Pixie De Costa. Staring at my nude body—her eyes hungry! Her hair like a wraith, caught upon the wind! Her every muscle taught and throbbing!

MARGOT: *(slightly confused.)* But we're on the fourteenth floor....

EMORY: In her drunkenness, she had climbed from YOUR balcony onto the ledge that runs the length of this outer wall and had positioned herself out side MY window, her robe flailing in the cold wet midnight air…Her breasts hanging limp and dejected… She had been staring at me while I slept….nude. She was ravishing me with her eyes, Miss Margot. All the while fingering the golden bowl of Aphrodite!!!

MARGOT: NO!

EMORY: It was horrible! Horrible! I screamed out a sound….a sound unlike any I had ever heard before…well, there was that one time in Mykynos, but never mind! I felt the chill of death run through me! Then suddenly, as if doused with ice cold water, Pixie shrieked to the heavens and flew back to your balcony, the ghostly pallor of her face disappearing into the swaths of these drapes. Miss Beezus swooned limply in my arms as I did the only thing I could do…..I vomited on the carpet. Rousing myself, as if from a nightmare, I tucked Miss Beezus away, washed my self off with warm, sudsy, lemon scented water and collapsed onto my bed……nude.

MARGOT: Oh, this is all my fault. She has been driven to this insanity! If it hadn't been for …the accident, Pixie would be a fine healthy girl with a family and friends and maybe even….dare I say….a church home.

EMORY: You mustn't blame yourself dear. She's the one that pushed you! And I saw it!

MARGOT: What? Saw what?

EMORY: In her eyes. The same thing you must have seen that horrible night so many years ago. The look of….death.

MARGOT: Oh, Emory….what am I to do?

EMORY: We must get Pixie away from here dear. She might hurt herself. She might hurt you! We'll find a nice, quite institution and have her taken care of by professionals. You know, ever since Olivia De Havilland made THE SNAKE PIT, I understand those places can be quite lovely now. They say Mayfair Regency Acres is perfectly ADORABLE. All of the really top notch Hollywood moguls desert their loved ones there! *(Meowing noises.)* And Miss Beezus agrees! Please consider it for Miss Pixie's well-being. And for your own.

MARGOT: Of course you are right Emory. I will try to be brave. You are such a dear friend.

(We hear Viddy entering.)

MARGOT: Sssh! Not a word to Viddy.

EMORY: I'm locked up tighter than Tab Hunters chinos....

VIDDY: Miss Margot, the mornin' is getting past us, and you haven't taken your pills yet...

MARGOT: Oh Viddy. Ever the mother hen.

(Viddy hands her the bottle of pills. Margot sets them absent-mindedly on the end table. She stares off, buried in thought.)

VIDDY: Mr. Emory, your sandwich is here.

EMORY: Thank you. Ooooo! You've removed the crust. You are a goddess on earth.

VIDDY: Miss Margot, where would you like your sandwich?

MARGOT: I'm not really hungry right now Viddy.

VIDDY: Well, you have to eat somethin'. The doctor ain't gonna be too happy if he finds out you ain't been eatin' right! And you simply have got to take them pills!

(A sudden outburst as Margot's composure snaps.)

MARGOT: Please! Can't you leave me alone! This bullying and clucking is driving me to madness! Madness I tell you! Get away from me! I can't bear the sight of either of you *(Pause.)* Oh please forgive me. I'd rather have cut off my right hand than have spoken to you that way. I know you are only thinking of me Viddy. My dearest companion. Please forgive me. I suddenly have this terrible headache.

EMORY: It's my fault, Viddy. I've been chattering away a mile a minute while our dear Miss Margot has graciously humored me.

MARGOT: It's just that you have given me so much to think about Emory. I think I'll go have a lie down.

EMORY: What a good idea! We'll have a nice long chat about THINGS later. When you are feeling better!

(Margot exits through bedroom door.)

EMORY: Poor Margot.

VIDDY: Mr. Emory, I have done worried myself half to death a-frettin' over Miss Margot. Its just terrible! And she's up half the night, rollin' that chair back and forth, sniffin' and cryin' and carryin' on somethin' fierce. All cause of Miss Pixie.

EMORY: Viddy. I have some very important news for you. I have contacted an institution for the mentally insane on Miss Margot's behalf.

VIDDY: For…?

EMORY: Yes, Darling. For Pixie! I have taken it upon myself to contact Mayfair Regency Acres in Santa Monica. They will be more than happy to look after Miss Pixie De Costa .

VIDDY: I don't know about that, Mr. Emory…

PIXIE: *(Offstage.)* HEY!

EMORY: There's the harpy now!

VIDDY: *(Calling off to Pixie.)* One moment Miss Pixie!

EMORY: It's the perfect set up Viddy! We'll let someone else shoulder the burden of that monster while you and Miss Margot live out your last, few, remaining years together. Alone and Content!

VIDDY: Mr. Emory….

PIXIE: *(Offstage.)* HEEEEEEEY!

VIDDY: Oh, lord. Miss Pixie will be wantin' her breakfast...

EMORY: Viddy please. We must keep even a whiff of this information away from Pixie.

VIDDY: Yes sir.

EMORY: One word, and our plan will be exposed.....NAKED for all the world to see!

VIDDY: Yes sir.

EMORY: For Miss Margot?

VIDDY: For Miss Margot.

(Emory and Viddy embrace.)

(Pixie, a disheveled drunken wreck enters. She is as sloppy as Margot is meticulous. Her face is remarkably similar to her sisters, but where Margot beams and radiates light, Pixie is twisted dark and ugly. Her platinum grey finger waved hair hangs limp, desperately holding on to past glories. She is slovenly, unkempt, and is barely contained inside a wild floral and marabou trimmed dressing gown. She doesn't walk but slouches along in her dirty pink mules.)

PIXIE: Dincha hear me CALLIN' for crissakes? HUH?

VIDDY: No ma'am. I was preparin' lunch for Mr. Emory and....your sister.

PIXIE: Oh yeah? And where is Miss Holier-than-thou?.

VIDDY: She took to bed with a headache.

PIXIE: Good. She can stay there for all I care. It'll be a swell break to not have to put up with that pain in the ass for awhile. *(Sees Emory.)* Who the hell are you?

EMORY: Emory Breedlove. I believe we have already met.

PIXIE: Oh yeah? Well what a treat for half of us.

(Miss Beezus mews.)

PIXIE: Crap on a crutch! You know you got a weasel chewin' on yer arm?

EMORY: Viddy I am afraid I must be going.

VIDDY: Yes Mister Emory.

EMORY: And remember Viddy. Not a WORD about what we discussed before. *(To PIXIE.)* It was a PLEASURE seeing you again Miss De Costa.

PIXIE: Are you still here?

EMORY: Of course. Au Revoir, Mam'selle Johnson!

(Emory and Miss Beezus leave.)

PIXIE: What the....? Who the hell is this Mam'selle Johnson?

VIDDY: *(Indignantly.)* I am! Johnson is my last name!

PIXIE: No kiddin'? Huh. Whattya know. Ya got a last name. Any mail yet?

VIDDY: No ma'am. None that I know of.

PIXIE: No mail today. No mail yestiddy. No mail EVER! Seems awful funny to me. Awful funny. I use to get THOUSANDS of letters a day from my fans! Little girls that wanted to grow up to be a great big star just like Pixie de Costa! I'd get marriage proposals in the mail , fer cryin' out loud! From foreign diplomats, crowned heads— Now nothin'…

VIDDY: Yes ma'am. You and Miss Margot were the toast of this here town, once upon a time.

PIXIE: Margot? MARGOT??? She was NEVER as loved as I was!! I practically CARRIED her to the top on the back of MY success! And what was my reward? A nice tidy life of suffering wrapped in a neat little box of heartache......I was the star! I was the star and don't you EVER forget it!

VIDDY: I ain't seen no mail today. Miss Pixie.

PIXIE: All right! Just see that ya hand it over to me when it gets here.

VIDDY: I always give Miss Margot the mail. There are important things for her to tend to. Bills and such.

PIXIE: And you think I'm too dumb to take care of any of that myself?

VIDDY: Maybe too drunk...

PIXIE: Look you. I'm about fed up, you get me?. Why are you always here? Every time I look up, there you are—judging me!

VIDDY: And I intend on staying here—as long as Miss Margot needs me. As long as you BOTH need me.

PIXIE: Well maybe we ain't gonna be needin' you after today...

VIDDY: What exactly do you mean by that, Miss Pixie.

PIXIE: I got plans, see? Big plans!

VIDDY: What you got on your mind?

PIXIE: No! I want it to be a surprise!

VIDDY: What kind of surprise Miss Pixie.

PIXIE: I'll tell you when I am good and ready! AFTER I have cinched the deal. And THEN you'll ALL see what a REAL STAR looks like. Now, I'm gonna go freshen up. I'm expecting company! HA!

(Pixie exits cackling maniacally.)

VIDDY: Company? Miss Pixie! Miss Pixie! Oh dear lord. What has that fool woman gone and done!

(Doorbell.)

MARGOT: *(Offstage.)* Viddy, would you see who that is?

VIDDY: Yes, Miss Margot! Lord, I feel like the very ground is shaking beneath my feet!

(Viddy answers door. It is Helena La Mancha, a vicious gossip columnist with the Los Angels Reporter, a less than reputable Tabloid. She wears a horrendous hat, gloves, bag and too-tight suit of the period. Like all woman of a certain age and position, she finds herself endlessly fascinating. Her sense of confidence is only outweighed by her sense of entitlement. The genteel persona she presents on the air belies the brash vulgarian she really is. She plows past Viddy straight into the room.)

HELENA: No need to show me in, dear. I know my way around this bird's nest. Good golly Marie! Look at this place! It hasn't changed a jot in 30 years! It is exactly as I remembered it from that horrible, horrible night!

VIDDY: Are you expected, miss...?

HELENA: La Mancha. Helena La Mancha. I am chief gossip columnist for the Los Angeles Reporter.

VIDDY: I don't believe we are entertaining guests today, Miss La Mancha.

HELENA: Oh, this isn't a casual little howdy-doo, honey. I'm here on business. Official SHOW business!

MARGOT: *(Offstage.)* Who is it Viddy?

VIDDY: A Miss La Mancha, Miss Margot. Helena La Mancha.

MARGOT: Oh, that horrible woman! Don't let her in Viddy!

HELENA: It's too late, sugar! As Marlon Brando once said to James Dean 'I'm already IN there, pal!'

(Margot enters.)

HELENA: Hello, Margot.

MARGOT: Helena. To what do we owe this rather distasteful surprise?

HELENA: Why Margot! You act as if you're not happy to see me!

MARGOT: Kit Cornell herself couldn't play that scene!

HELENA: I'm crushed!

MARGOT: Well, what do you expect? For years you have tormented Pixie and myself with the lies and innuendo you spew in that filthy rag of a newspaper you write for! Why couldn't you have left us alone?

HELENA: Well, you know it HAD to be something big to get me all the way up here. It's something I thought you should know! I'd just HATE myself if I didn't tell you all about it.

MARGOT: What are you talking about, Helena?

HELENA: Just a little tip that came my way. It's such a live wire that it practically CRAWLED across my desk! The other morning I happened to receive, in the mail, a trade swap advertising for a script doctor. A little tidbit someone sends in to me, in hopes that I'll run it in my column. *(Takes out the letter.)* Seems some dried up piece of horseflesh is trying to find a sap writer who is down on their luck enough to ghost-write for them. Who cares, right? I'm getting' ready to toss it—and then I noticed the signature.

MARGOT: I don't see what any of this has to do with me.

HELENA: "Wanted: Handsome and Virile Male Scriptwriter willing to work on Grand Return Project with Major Star. Must be well built, Heterosexual and carry his own typewriter! Signed—Pixie De Costa"

MARGOT: *(Thunderstruck.)* P - Pixie - ?

HELENA: Seems your sisters plannin' on makin' a big comeback! You wanna give me the poop before the scoop?

VIDDY: Miss La Mancha, I think it is time for you to leave.

HELENA: You'll call off the attack dog, if you know what's good for ya, Miss De Costa! Well, what's good for you AND your sister....

VIDDY: Miss Margot

MARGOT: Its alright Viddy. Perhaps you could whip up a batch of your famous tomato juice frappes for Miss La Mancha and myself.

VIDDY: Yes Miss Margot.

MARGOT: Only not so much salt dear. Salt does the most horrible things to slugs....

(Viddy exits.)

HELENA: That's more like it.

MARGOT: Helena, I don't see what could possibly interest you in....

HELENA: Are you kiddin' me? OH, you are a RIOT, you are! Funnier than Milton Berle! For twenty-five years, you and Pixie have been stowed away up here, safe from a world that wants to ask too many questions. Quite a cozy little arrangement. I wonder how many toddies that WEREN'T as notorious as your sister could have dodged an attempted murder rap the way Pixie did?

MARGOT: Helena please! Pixie was cleared of all wrong-doing in... the accident. And she has been nothing more than content to see to my every need...

HELENA: Well, it seems that 'seeing to your every need' just isn't enough anymore. It looks like Pixie De Costa is stepping OUT! And in no time, the world is gonna want to know just what exactly has been goin' on up here on the 14th floor ! What sickness, what perversion, what madness, has been fermenting away up here far from the heat of the spotlight. And a lot of hack writers less credible than I will write all Sorts of lies and distortions! They'll finger this place for an opium den, with you and Pixie starring as the cocaine fueled madams of your own white slavery ring. Or they'll say how CLOSE you and Pixie have become over the years with no man around. VERY close! TOO CLOSE FOR SISTERS, if you get my drift.

MARGOT: Stop it Helena! Stop it! Stop it!

HELENA: Aw, un-snap your girdle, Margot. You know I don't go in for any of that yellow journalism crap! I got my integrity to think about! For 25 years this story has been a cold fish. And now—finally—it looks like Pixie De Costa is ready to heat things up!

MARGOT: What—exactly—is it that you want Helena?

HELENA: I want the goods, Margot. I want the story. And I want it first. I want to blast the news across the front page so big and so bold that the other rags in this town won't even know what hit 'em! Because you are gonna give me the item to end all items...you and your ...sister. Pixie has opened the door and I'm taking the first step in! I can see the headline now. Letters four inches tall and two inches thick 'LOOK WHAT'S HAPPENED TO PIXIE DE COSTA'.

MARGOT: I think I am going to be physically ill.

HELENA: Yeah, I'm even startin' to make MYSELF a little sick!

MARGOT: It has always been a great mystery to me, Helena, how creatures like you are allowed to roam the streets of Hollywood. Hollywood—where life is good and decent and pure! Where every man is a red blooded patriot and every woman is the girl next door. Dreams are created here Helena, not the nightmares that you concoct!

HELENA: Save the hearts and flowers, will ya? When are you gonna wake up and face the facts? The fantasy is over! This is 1957 and the American public ain't buyin' your line of make believe anymore! There are communists hiding around every corner! Fluoride is being dumped into the drinking water! And it looks like Ricky wasn't so crazy about Lucy AFTER all!

MARGOT: You are a despicable and loathsome perversion of everything that MAKES a woman, Helena. Your cruelty has erased any last vestige of femininity from you. Why, you are almost mannish! I feel SORRY for you!

HELENA: Look you might as well spill! If I don't get it from you, I'll get it from Pixie!

MARGOT: THEN GET IT FROM PIXIE! I'm sure you won't be disappointed! Now If you will excuse me. There are a few prayers that need to be said!

(Margot exits. Helena looks around. Viddy enters with tray of tomato juice frappes.)

VIDDY: Where is Miss Margot?

MARGOT: I believe she has gone to do the rosary at the porcelain altar!

(Doorbell.)

VIDDY: Now who could that be?

(Doorbell.)

HELENA: Oooh! Maybe this is Billy Wilder now! Funny. If he's carrying a type-writer, I wonder what he's ringing the doorbell with.

VIDDY: What? Who? Who? What?

PIXIE: *(Offstage.)* HEEEEEEY! Answer the damn door will ya? For cryin' out loud!

HELENA: I'll just sit over here and make myself at home.

VIDDY: Miss La Mancha…

(Doorbell.)

PIXIE: *(Offstage.)* HEEEEEEEEEEEEEEEEEEEEEEEEYYYYY!!!!

VIDDY: All right! All right! I'll answer the damned door!

(Viddy exits to answer the front door. Helena looks around the room.)

HELENA: Calm yourself Helena. It looks like your long wait is about to pay off. While it's true that a watched pot never boils, soup left simmering can burn down the plantation.

(Eddie enters followed by Viddy. Eddie is a real tough guy, being chased half way across the country by his demons. Burnt out, disappointed, angry, and suspicious are his GOOD qualities. Will do anything to make a buck. Take Bogey, Cagney and Robinson. Mix them up with a fifth of whiskey then run him over with Mike Hammers car. That's Eddie. Wears a suit and tie. Carries a coat and fedora.)

VIDDY: I don't understand. Was Miss Margot expecting you?

EDDIE: I don't know nothin' about a Margot, kid. I'm here about an ad in Variety. Some broad says she's lookin' for a writer to punch up some kinda script she's workin' on…

VIDDY: I am not sure we are receiving today.

EDDIE: That's tough, kid. 'Cause I'm here to deliver.

HELENA: I bet you are…

EDDIE: Who's the fruit bowl?

PIXIE: *(Offstage.)* VIIIIIIIIIIIIIIIIDDY! Get in here!

VIDDY: Lord Jesus.

(Viddy exits.)

HELENA: So you're here in answer to Miss De Costa's ad?

EDDIE: Who are you, J. Edgar Hoover's more masculine sister?

HELENA: No. Just an interested friend you might say. And now that you're here, that interest has piqued!

EDDIE: Ya know, that line wouldn't work coming from a dame half your age.....

HELENA: And what lines DO work, Mr.....?

EDDIE: Grant. Eddie Grant.

HELENA: Like Ulysses. How Greek.

EDDIE: Look, doll. If I wanted a pick up, I'd call a garbage truck. No offense baby.

HELENA: None taken....baby. This won't be the first time I've been called trash.

EDDIE: And you can bet your rubber ass it won't be the last time either, sweetheart.

HELENA: You're pretty tough, for a script jockey. Ad says she's lookin' for a hetero writer. You a straight-shooter, cowboy?

EDDIE: I ain't never had any complaints.

HELENA: I'll bet. Care for a frappe?

EDDIE: I don't drink nothin' this time a day that ain't 100 proof. Got any gin?

(Helena takes a flask out of her bag.)

HELENA: I never leave home without it.

EDDIE: Like a regular boy scout huh? Always prepared…

(Helena rubs up against Eddie.)

HELENA: Absolutely. A girl never knows what kind of HARDship she's gonna come up against….

EDDIE: Or what kinda HARDship she's gonna create…

HELENA: I wonder what you could mean.

EDDIE: I wonder if you wonder….

HELENA: So what's a big strapping handsome mook like you doin' down on his luck? Ain't you the guy with the stuff that dreams are made on? Why isn't some wealthy old dye-job lavishing you with expensive gifts?

EDDIE: Lets just say that I've had a lot of mistresses in my life, baby, but none that did a number on me like Lady Mary Jane…

HELENA: Ah, so you're a dope fiend.

EDDIE: Former.

HELENA: What made ya kick? Love of a good woman?

EDDIE: I had plenty of red flags waving in my face, like that one time after a six day bender I came to wearing a leather bikini while I was being used as a piñata at an all male lingerie party.

HELENA: Wish I had been a fly on that wall…

EDDIE: The Dope made me stupid. Too stupid to work. Instead of writing, I'd spend all my time chasin' no class dead end dames like you…

HELENA: And those days are gone? You give up the chase?

EDDIE: Oh I get the itch every now and then, but then I remember how much I hate myself when I wake up with a wrong number that smells like the urinal in a frat house.

HELENA: You got the sweetest little way of turnin' a lady's head.

EDDIE: Go find me a lady, and we'll try out your theory.

HELENA: You don't think much of me, do you?

EDDIE: Baby, I'm tryin' not to think about you at all.

(Pixie and Viddy enter. Pixie has made herself somewhat more presentable. She wears a dress from the twenties, Pink silk with buttons and flowers. It is a sad attempt to look younger and more appealing. In Pixies dusty mind it works! In reality, not so much…)

PIXIE: I am SOOO sorry for makin' ya wait so long. I wasn't finished dressin'. And Beauty is a cruel mistress…

EDDIE: Yeah. It looks like she smacked the hell of out of ya.…

PIXIE: HELENA!

HELENA: Pixie, DARLING!!!

(They 'fake Hollywood' embrace.)

HELENA: I hope you don't mind me crashing your little get together. But when I read the ad I practically jumped for joy! Why, this is the biggest news since Joan Crawford left Metro! It's the surprise of the century!

PIXIE: Of course I don't mind. We're gonna need all the publicity we can get! Any mention in your column is gonna be big for me and.…I'm sorry. WE haven't met.

EDDIE: The names Grant. Eddie Grant.

PIXIE: Oh I like the sound of that! It's so...rugged. *(She shudders.)* Oh dear! Forgive me Mister Grant! I just had the oddest sensation! Sort of a thrill that raced across my soul! Do you believe in fate, Mr. Grant? I was doin' my charts the other day. It seems that Capricorn is in retrograde and Cancer is in Uranus. *(Eddie looks at his ass.)* What I am saying, Mr. Grant, is that our meeting was predestined by the stars! The universe ordained this! And I just know that this is the beginning of a beautiful friendship.

(End of Act One.)

ACT II

PIXIE: Where are my manners! Viddy take the gentleman's hat.

VIDDY: Yes Ma'am

EDDIE: Thanks, kid.

PIXIE: And could you rustle up some lemonade. And maybe some of them thumb-print cookies we got in there?

VIDDY: Miss Pixie I don't think…

PIXIE: *(Through clenched teeth.)* Do what I'm tellin' ya!

VIDDY: Lord Jesus….

(Viddy leaves.)

PIXIE: Won't you sit down Mr. Grant? Here! Next to me. Now. Ain't this nice?

EDDIE: between this and a shot in the nuts, I'd take the shot…

PIXIE: Won't you tell me a little about yourself Mr. Grant?

EDDIE: What's to tell? I been knockin' around Hollywood for about 10 years. Lookin' for my big break. 10 years in and I'm still lookin'. I saw your ad and said what the hell. I got nuthin' else goin' on so here I am.

PIXIE: Well! How persuasive! Would I know any of your work?

EDDIE: I doubt it. I wasted most of my life and talent knockin'out grade Z fillers that run at Times Square grind-houses at two-thirty in the morning. Stuff where the main guy is framed for murder and slugs a big busted blonde before the end of the first reel. Crap any bargain basement hack with a typewriter woulda turned down 'cause they still had a shred of dignity. That, and a lot of V. D. films for the Navy.

PIXIE: How...vivid....Helena, I think you can skip this part.

HELENA: Right.

EDDIE: So what's the job? I ain't got all day...

(Viddy enters with tray of drinks and cookies.)

VIDDY: Miss Pixie, I must speak with you in the other room...

PIXIE: Later...dear.

EDDIE: Look, Lady. I'm growin' old here.

PIXIE: Well, Mr. Grant. I can see that you have certainly put in your time in the trenches. So, I am going to offer you the biggest break of your career. Of course, you know who I am...

(He stares at her blankly.)

PIXIE: I am Pixie De Costa!

EDDIE: What the hell is a Pixie De Costa?

PIXIE: Helena, you can skip this part too. I am one of the leading movie actresses in Hollywood. Only I haven't made a picture in...well... sometime.

HELENA: 25 years! Isn't that exciting?

PIXIE: Helena! Mr. Grant, It has become painfully clear to me that I can no longer deny my fans the face and voice that they've been craving. I feel the demand for my reappearance on screen must be met!

EDDIE: So you are talking about a comeback...

PIXIE: No! Not a comeback! I HATE that word! I never left! It will be a return!

A return to the former glory of my career before…things happened. A triumphant return to the art form that has so desperately needed me. My selfish withdrawal must end so that the world may know again the GLORY THAT IS PIXIE DE COSTA!!!!

EDDIE: What's the pay?

PIXIE: What?

EDDIE: You heard me. How much?

PIXIE: Well…I don't really know…how do they usually…?

VIDDY: Miss Pixie…

PIXIE: Viddy, why don't you go out to the kitchen and whip up a batch of your banana puddin' while we're talkin' business?

VIDDY: Lord Jesus *(Viddy exits.)*

PIXIE: Now where were we?

EDDIE: I'll take 250 bucks up front and 50 bucks every week till we're through. You're gonna hand me another 400 bucks when I am finished. On top of that, I'll need 25 dollars cash and a pack of Lucky's every day—per diem.

PIXIE: Helena?

HELENA: Take it honey! Take it! The world can NOT be denied your artistry any longer!

PIXIE: You're right! It's all for them! Those wonderful people out there in the dark!

EDDIE: So you gonna let me look at this stiff I'm suppose to be punchin' up?

PIXIE: Of course! It's right here! I've been working on it off and on for a few years.

HELENA: 25 years! Isn't that unimaginable?

EDDIE: What's unimaginable is that this sack of flesh can actually spell.

(Pixie crosses to the desk and pulls out a manuscript the size of a phone book. She drops the script into Eddies Lap.)

EDDIE: Hey! Careful Lady. I was hopin' to use that again some day!

HELENA: Good lord Pixie! What is it!

PIXIE: It's the story of a lifetime Helena. A story only a great artist can tell!

(Viddy enters with banana pudding. She sets the tray down.)

VIDDY: Miss Pixie, WE HAVE GOT TO TALK!

PIXIE: Viddy darling, got any cheese and crackers out there?

VIDDY: Lord Jesus *(Viddy exits.)*

HELENA: Go on Pixie. I'm all a twitter! Aren't you, Mr. Grant?

EDDIE: I don't twitter. If your lucky. I'll just fart a little…

PIXIE: ANYWAY! Every great actress has at least once in her career tackled the story of a great historical figure. It has brought them notoriety and fame. Norma Shearer had Marie Antoinette. Garbo did Queen Christina, Dietrich was the Scarlet Empress. Hell, even that bitch Greer Garson stole Madame Currie right out from under me!

HELENA: The injustice.

EDDIE: Maybe a needle full of Clorox would take care of all this….

PIXIE: Well now, its my turn! I will bring to the screen the greatest Motion Picture

Biography since The Great Ziegfeld. For my part I will essay a role that will capture lightening in a bottle. I will portray the one woman of this century that changed the course of history like no other!

HELENA: Oh Pixie! Tell us! Who will it be???

PIXIE: TYPHOID MARY!

HELENA: How divine!

EDDIE: Holy Crap!

HELENA: I can't believe that nobody had thought of this before!

PIXIE: It will not only be MY greatest triumph, but the worlds!

HELENA: May I quote you?

PIXIE: But wait! There's more!

HELENA: Is it possible?

EDDIE: Ain't this enough?

PIXIE: Not only will the role of Typhoid Mary herald the return of Pixie De Costa to the world of cinema where she can resume her proper place amongst the stars. But…!

HELENA: Yes?

PIXIE: It …Will…Be…

HELENA: Yes? YES?

PIXIE: A MUSICAL!!!!!!!!!

HELENA: Dear God!

EDDIE: I musta left my gun in the cab…

PIXIE: Yes the heart and soul of a woman cursed with a disfiguring and gruesome disease …mixed with some really great tunes we can get Dinah Shore to record later! It cannot miss!

HELENA: It's a natural.

(Viddy enters with tray of Cheese and crackers. She slams the tray down.)

VIDDY: Here are you're damn cheese and crackers! Now, Miss Pixie….

PIXIE: I think we're gonna need some coffee for after Viddy!

VIDDY: We are runnin' out of trays!

PIXIE: *(Screaming.)* DO WHAT I'M TELLIN' YA!

VIDDY: Lord Jesus…

(Viddy exits.)

PIXIE: Now Mr. Grant…or may I call you…Eddie. Does my little production…attract you?

EDDIE: Typhoid Mary or Mary queen of Scots, who gives a rat's ass in a snowstorm! I couldn't care less if this wad of typing was about Queen Victoria's first PERIOD! I haven't eaten anything but butter and ketchup sandwiches for a month. So pay up, ya crazy cow! I'll take this pile of crap home, read it, think of a good reason not to slash my throat with a broken beer bottle, and get back to you.

(He stands and holds out his hand. Pixie misunderstanding caresses it to her bosom.)

PIXIE: Oh Eddie. How forceful you are. It gives a girl ideas!

EDDIE: Girl? Don't look now, but ya got a little crazy hangin' off your chin.

PIXIE: Eddie, could we be alone? There are some details I'd like to work out.

EDDIE: No. I'd like you to take your tit out of my hand and replace it with a check. 250 bucks up front. I'll go ahead and take the first couple of days per diem too.

PIXIE: Why yes. Yes of course.

(Pixie crosses to desk and writes check.)

PIXIE: Isn't this exciting? Helena, I hope you're taking all of this down!

HELENA: I'm not missing a word!

PIXIE: Here you are, Eddie. Take it and return to me soon. I place the fate of Mary and in some ways, Pixie in your capable hands.

EDDIE: Right. I'll stop by again tomorrow. Have some gin waitin'. And some morphine.

(Eddie leaves. Pixie follows to the door.)

PIXIE: Oh Helena. Could you ever have imagined that it would have gone so well.

HELENA: That ain't the half of it kid.

PIXIE: Helena. May I tell ya somethin'? Strictly off the record?

(Viddy enters.)

HELENA: Of course doll face!

PIXIE: I'm in love!

HELENA: No!

PIXIE: Yes! I'm in love with Eddie Grant! Oh, I know it sounds crazy. Absurd! Mad! But that's what love is...an absurd sort of mad craziness. When we touched there was...electricity! I'm sure you could feel it too!

HELENA: Of course, dear. One would have to be DEAD not to be aware of the animal heat being generated between the two of you.

PIXIE: Oh Helena, you are happy for me, ain't ya?

HELENA: I am ECSTATIC! Well, my darling Pixie. I must go! You can expect a LENGTHY treatise in the my column tomorrow. I may come back later to take a few photographs. Go glamorous so we can sell the part! Call Edith Head! I'm sure she could put you in something that just screams typhus!

PIXIE: Oh Helena. Do we girls deserve to feel this much love?

HELENA: Of Course dear. Especially when we are BOTH getting EXACTLY what we want. Ta-ta for now!

(Helena exits. Pixie, lost in a world of romance, stares off into the distance.)

PIXIE: Eddie Grant. Mrs. Eddie Grant. Mrs. Pixie De Costa Grant! *(To Heaven.)* Oh daddy! I'm so happy!

VIDDY: Miss Pixie......

PIXIE: Get the hell outta here will ya?

VIDDY: But....

PIXIE: Get out!

VIDDY: Lord Jesus!

(Viddy exits grumbling all the way.)

PIXIE: Oh, papa! It's all starting to happen. I'm gonna be the happiest girl in the whole wide world! Nothin' can stand in my way! *(Suddenly thinks of Margot)* Only, I gotta take care of one minor detail first.

(Pixie looks off in Margot's direction as the music swells ominously and the lights fade to a foreboding black.)

NEWSBOY: Hey! Wait! Stop! Cheese and rice!

VIDDY: Hold on there a minute, boy! What you doin'?

NEWSBOY: That screw-loose is gonna kill Margot! We gotta do somethin'!

VIDDY: Child, you talkin' crazy!!

NEWSBOY: We gotta save her!

VIDDY: WE don't gotta do nothin'! We can't! All these things already happened. These are but shadows of things come and gone...

NEWSBOY: But...

VIDDY: No buts! You want to change things you got no power over? You wanna cure Judith Traherne of blindness? You wanna invite Stella Dallas to the wedding? Do you wanna pull Ilsa Lund off that plane in Casablanca?

NEWSBOY: So you're just gonna stand by and get your heart broken all over again??

VIDDY: Yes. Yes I am. And it sure enough did break my heart. You know I loved Miss Margot. Loved her like a sister. And she loved me right back. And if I could, knowing what I do, well.....maybe things would have turned out better. But all the love in the world, and all your hoping and wishing, can't undo what's already done... Later that night, Miss Pixie took a sharp turn for the worse.....and every damn one of us paid for it.....

(Lights come up on the Penthouse hours after the previous action. It is deep into the night now. Pixie stumbles into the room with a fringed shawl draped over one shoulder. She carries a picture of her father and a half empty bottle of Jim Beam. She has

been drinking.)

PIXIE: Was there ever a better papa ever in the whole wide world?

So many people ask me, where did you get your smile?
Your curly hair, your rosy cheeks, your talent to beguile?
I tell them, 'Why an Angel…who lives in clouds above!
Each day he watches over me and showers me with love.
He kisses me with sunshine and a soft and gentle breeze.
He wipes away my tears when I get boo boos on my knees
And when the world is less then kind and makes me feel all sad
My white knight from above appears. My champion. My Dad…
Oh papa….

HENRY: Pixie honey? It's me! Papa!

PIXIE: Papa? Is that you?

HENRY: Yes I just said it was. Sugar beet, I've returned to you from heaven to deliver a very important message!

PIXIE: Where ya been Papa?

HENRY: I just told you. Heaven.

PIXIE: And why are you here?

HENRY: Am I speaking French? I am here to deliver…

PIXIE: Papa? Is that you?

HENRY: Oh, for cryin' out loud, would you just shut up and listen for a minute? Jeez. I have crossed over from the great beyond to bring my shiny little star to her destiny!

PIXIE: Is this someone I know, papa?

HENRY: You've never been very bright, have you honey?

PIXIE: My dress is pretty!

HENRY: Right. Look, you are gonna get everything you want, baby. And soon. All ya gotta do is get rid of the lead weight in the wheelchair…

PIXIE: What wheelchair?

HENRY: I swear to God your mother must have stood too close to the kerosene cooker when she was pregnant with you. I'm talking about Margot!

PIXIE: Are you talking about Margot, Papa?

HENRY: Yes! Margot! I would shoot myself if I weren't already dead…Look, ya gotta wipe out Margot! And after you have pitched her cold dead carcass into the Pacific, think how you life can change! You'll have friends again! You'll give parties again! You might even get to bone that stiff in the rented monkey suit!

PIXIE: Eddie! My Eddie!

HENRY: Right! Now be a good girl and go kill your sister…

PIXIE: Goodbye Papa!

HENRY: Make daddy proud!

PIXIE: I will. Papa! Wait! What's heaven like?

HENRY: Perfect honey! No Worries. No Cares. No Catholics….And I haven't seen your mother since 1927….See ya soon, honey bear! Really, really…..really soon!

PIXIE: I miss you! I miss you! I love you…….

(Pixie cries softly as Viddy enters the room. She has finished cleaning up all the trays and food and has come back to finish her conversation with Pixie. She's startled to see Pixie so vulnerable.)

VIDDY: Miss Pixie?

PIXIE: PAPA?????

VIDDY: Uh…..no…..

PIXIE: Oh. Its you. Did you finish cleanin' up? I don't want this place lookin' like a sty when my friends come back….

VIDDY: I don't like this Miss Pixie! I don't like it one bit!

PIXIE: Who cares? Nobody's askin' you.

VIDDY: No they ain't! But there also ain't a chance in the world that Miss Margot is gonna allow you to do what you are plannin' on doin'!

PIXIE: Is that so? Well I got news for you, I want you out. Do ya here me? Out!!!

VIDDY: Miss Pixie, I still got work to do! It ain't even 9:00 yet!

PIXIE: I don't care! Yer fired! Get out!

VIDDY: Miss Pixie…

PIXIE: I'll give ya just two minutes to grab yer crap and clear out, or I'll call the cops!! They'll run yer ass in. I'll tell 'em some crazy bitch has broken into my house and has threatened me! And they'll believe every word I say….cuz I am a famous movie star. And who are you? A nothin'! A nobody!

VIDDY: And I think you'd do it too! Just out of meanness! Well, my momma didn't raise no fool. I guess I'll be goin'

PIXIE: And I'll take yer front door key.

VIDDY: ER—uh—I don't have it with me. Miss Margot let me in this morning. I must have left it at home in my other bag.

PIXIE: Whatta dope. I'll change the locks tomorrow. Now get out of here before I tear yer eyes out.

VIDDY: *(One last try)* I wanna say good bye to Miss Margot.

PIXIE: Just move yer ass and get lost!

(Viddy Leaves.)

(Pixie wipes her brow. She looks down at the bottle of pills and gets an idea.)

PIXIE: Now then, there's something I need to take care of…

(She goes into Margot's room. We hear the sister's conversation from off stage.)

PIXIE: Wake up Margot! Are these your pills?

MARGOT: Why yes. I need to take them. What was all of that noise?

PIXIE: It was Viddy. She showed her ass, so I fired her.

MARGOT: What?

(Pixie comes back into the room and talks through the door to Margot.)

PIXIE: You heard me. Hey! Just stay put! I don't want you rollin' out here and getting in my way. I'll get you somethin' to wash down these pills.

(Pixie goes about the room finding every booze bottle that she has hidden away. She mixes up a god awful drink in a glass.)

PIXIE: Ya know things are gonna be different around this dump from now on. I'm gonna run this joint like a battleship. Hey! No back talk! When I say hop yer gonna *(thinks about it)* well, ya ain't gonnna hop are ya. Cause yer in that chair! Ya are in that chair, ain't ya? Huh? Huh? Whatsa matter, Margot? CAT GOT YOUR TONGUE? I don't need Viddy or anybody else bossin' me around. I can boss myself.

(Pixie exits through upstage archway to the Kitchen. We hear she and Margot continue their conversation.)

MARGOT: Who was that man that was here earlier?

PIXIE: Wouldn't you just love to know?

MARGOT: I have a right to know who comes into my own home!

(Pixie enters again with huge box of rat poison and dumps it into Margot's drink. As she continues her conversation, she empties the entire contents of Margot's pills into the drink.)

PIXIE: Oh sure ya do! You just have to know everything, don't you? Well for Your information that was the Handsome Mr. Eddie Grant! And he was here to see ME! ONLY ME! A real screenwriter, not like them hacks YOU used to work with! He is gonna help me get my script together for the BIG picture I'm gonna be makin'! That's right sister dear! He's here for me! Me! And I can tell already that he's interested in me for more than just my talent! We might even get MARRIED someday! How would you like that?

(She exits into Margot's room.)

MARGOT: Well, I think that would be WONDERFUL Pixie!

PIXIE: Oh, ya do...

MARGOT: Yes I have only ever wanted you to be happy

(Pixie begins to laugh and reenters the room.)

PIXIE: Me? Happy? That's all you ever wanted? You are killin' me. *(Her laughter dies.)* Killin' me for sure with that one.

(Suddenly we see a vulnerability in Pixie and a reality that we haven't seen before. It is a glimpse of the woman Pixie is under the layers of anger.)

PIXIE: You want me happy. Of all the vicious hateful lies you ever told me, Margot De Costa, this is the worst. You wanted me happy? When was that? When the studio snatched you up and groomed you for the career I shoulda had? Is that when you wanted me happy? Or was it the night that you rubbed it in my face so hard we ended up on that balcony.....that lousy, stinkin' balcony. Was that to make me happy? No, Margot. I got a friend now. A true friend. He's gonna make me happy. And really, when you think about it, there is only one way YOU can truly make me happy. *(With deep terrible meaning)* Go on Margot. Take... yer... medicine

MARGOT: But Pixie!

PIXIE: Do it Margot!

MARGOT: But Pixie!

PIXIE: Drink it Margot! That's right. Drink it all down. Like a good girl. Alllllllllll gooooooonnnneee! Now get some sleep.

(She deliberately closes Margot's door, locking it. Pixie suddenly looks up and moves toward center stage as if in a trance.)

PIXIE: Papa?....Papa? Are you there, Papa? I did it Papa. I did it....All of it...The pills...The Poison...The fall....All of it! And I promise you this Papa! I will make you proud of me at last because I WILL BE A STAR....AGAIN!

(Pixie turns and flies out of the room. Just then we here the jingle of keys at the front door. Very stealthily, Viddy peeks around the archway. She looks around and creeps into the room. She tucks her house key into her purse.)

VIDDY: That's right Miss De Costa! Momma didn't raise no fool!

(Viddy looks around and sees that the coast is clear. Then she goes to the balcony to make sure that it is deserted. Next, Viddy hurry's over to look toward Pixies room. She decides that she is safe. She goes to Margot's bedroom door and starts to open it. Only the door won't open. It is locked!)

VIDDY: What the...? This door is locked! We NEVER lock these doors! Lord have mercy! What has she done? What has she done? Miss Margot? Miss Margot? Are you in there? Can you hear me? Oh, what has she done!!! Miss Margot you sit tight for a minute!

(Viddy runs to the desk and picks up the phone and dials.)

VIDDY: Hello, Police Station? Yes, I need to speak with Detective Michael O'Halleran please! Its an emergency! *(Pause.)* Detective O'Halleran? This is Miss Vivian Johnson over at the De Costa Apartment. Yes sir! That's right! You need to get over here right away! It looks like our worst nightmares are comin' true! Hurry!

(She hangs up the phone and reaches into the desk and pulls out a hammer and screwdriver.)

VIDDY: Good thing we always keep this hammer and screwdriver in the desk!

(Viddy returns to the door and starts to pound on the hinges to take the door off. As she hammers, Pixie enters through the archway, dressed again in her robe, and stands looking at Viddy in horror.)

VIDDY: I swear to God, Miss Margot! If anything has happened to you, I'll never forgive myself! Oh, please be all right! Oh, please be all right!

PIXIE: What are YOU doin' back here? I thought I told you to get out!

VIDDY: Well it just so happens that I only take my orders from Miss Margot! Now why is this door locked?

PIXIE: I don't have to tell you anything!

VIDDY: Miss Pixie, you know that the doctor has said a hundred times that these doors are to stay unlocked! Now you give me the key!

PIXIE: No! I don't wanna!

(Viddy puts the hammer down on the fireplace and advances toward Pixie.)

VIDDY: You give me that key and stop all this foolishness. Miss Pixie, you are a grown woman and it is time you start actin' like one! Now you GIVE ME THAT

KEY!

PIXIE: It's on the desk.

(Viddy crosses to the desk and gets the key. While her Back is turned, Pixie picks up the Hammer and advances on Viddy...)

VIDDY: I swear to you, when I get that door open, you, me AND Miss Margot are gonna sit down and have a long talk. Then I am callin' your doctor....

PIXIE: I can't let ya do that Viddy,

> *(Viddy turns and is startled to see Pixie wielding a hammer at her.)*

VIDDY: Miss Pixie!

> *(Pixie advances on Viddy and backs her up across the room.)*

PIXIE: I can't let ya do that Viddy. Ya see that doctor is sooooooo mean. He's not very nice to me. He's tryin' to get rid of me! For years and years he's tried to get rid of me...

VIDDY: Miss Pixie, please! Miss Margot! Miss Margot!

PIXIE: Miss Margot can't hear you anymore Viddy. In fact Nobody's gonna be able to hear you anymore. Because your voice...will...be...SILENCED!!

VIDDY: NOOO!!

(By now Pixie has backed Viddy offstage left behind the archway. Pixie raises the hammer and beats Viddy to death accompanied by a wild Bernard Herrmann score! The violence takes place out of sight to the audience but the wildness and fury in Pixies face should tell the whole story. When Viddy is sufficiently dead, all that we can see are her orthopedic oxfords sticking out from behind the archway. Pixie drops the hammer, goes to the sofa, grabs a throw and places it over Viddy. Pixie staggers back into the room, exhilarated.)

PIXIE: So much for a severance package....

(The doorbell rings! Pixie freezes.)

PIXIE: Oh no....Retribution comes swiftly!

(The doorbell rings again! Then there's a knock at the door.)

EDDIE: Hey! Open up! Its Eddie!

(Pixie immediately brightens.)

PIXIE: Eddie!!

(She flies out of the room and lets Eddie in. They enter through the Archway. Eddie still has the script...)

EDDIE: I forgot my hat..

PIXIE: I'm so glad you come back Eddie. I been thinkin' about ya ever since ya left! And ya know, its just so funny, us just havin' met and all, me thinkin' about ya so much...

EDDIE: Right. My hat in here?

(He opens the closet.)

PIXIE: But maybe it's not so funny after all. I mean people connect, ya know? Even if they never ever met before. Like we did. Like we connected!

EDDIE: Whattya talkin' about, ya crazy dame....

PIXIE: I'm talkin' about us!

EDDIE: Us? There ain't no us!

PIXIE: Ah, don't fight it Eddie. I know you feel it. I know you do! The second you walked in here today I just knew it was like DESTINY! We were meant to be together! You can give me back my career....I can give you a warm body waitin' in your bed every night.

EDDIE: You really are nuts! Look lady, I'm a recovering dope fiend that needs a pay check, not some two bit hustler lookin' for a five dollar screw! I gotta monkey on my back, baby, I don't need one hangin' off my front!

PIXIE: But Eddie! Don't you find me ...desirable?

EDDIE: Toots, I'm sure at one time the thought of you gave every Joe in a trench coat a jolt to the Johnson. Now you wouldn't encourage wood in a necrophilia...

PIXIE: I still got my looks!

EDDIE: Well, maybe you oughta trade 'em in for a newer model!

PIXIE: Is it someone else? Have you found someone else? Who is she? I'll scratch her eyes out!!

EDDIE: I need you to get the hell out of my way!

(He shoves Pixie out of the way.)

EDDIE: That's all I need is another tired, sagging, rickets-ridden, puss bag trying to take a swing on my schwantz!

(He opens the closet and is reaching for his hat. Meantime, Pixie has scooped up the screwdriver and with one sharp blow, sinks it into the warm muscular flesh between Eddies shoulders and jerks the screwdriver back out. He stumbles and turns to Pixie. He chokes as he dies.)

EDDIE: Wait! I ain't sore at ya kid! You done me a favor! I have been looking for a way to do it myself for a long time, only I'm too yella. Now gimme one more. Right here. The empty spot where my heart use to be.

(Stunned, Pixie raises the screwdriver into the air and with a shriek, plunges it into

Eddies chest.)

EDDIE: Sorry kid. It woulda been —swell...

(He cries out and collapses into the closet. DEAD!)

PIXIE: Oh Eddie. Why? Why? Why do you make me do these horrible things to you? I never wanted to hurt you Eddie! But ya made me! YA MADE ME!!! Papa! Papa! Make all the killing STOP!!!

(Chip calls from off stage.)

CHIP: Hello? Maintenance!

PIXIE: No! Must be quiet! Must be quiet! Must be quiet!!!

CHIP: I come up to see about an electrical socket?

PIXIE: Its not such a good time right now really...

CHIP: It'll only take a minute. Hey! Did you know your front door was open...?

(Chip wanders in. He is a gorgeous hunky young man of about 22 with bright eyes and a sparkle in his smile. He is dressed in tight jeans and Marlon Brando Tee-Shirt. Pixie slams the closet door closed and turns to Chip. She is stunned by his beauty.)

PIXIE: What are you.....? Why come in....young man. Young....young....young.... man.

CHIP: Sorry, ma'am. Is this a good time?

PIXIE: I'll give it my best shot! Please excuse the way I'm dressed...or undressed. It seems you have me at a disadvantage. I feel very vulnerable.

CHIP: Oh I'll be outta your hair in no time.

PIXIE: Good. The sooner to get you IN to OTHER places

CHIP: Is this the offending outlet?

PIXIE: Lets hope.

CHIP: I'll just remove the outer covering and dig around in its guts for a second. That should tell me if there is any spark left. Zowie, there sure is a lot of steam comin' out of this little box! Sometimes if the raw wires rub up against each other, they can create quite a fire! The heat can be so intense, that the interior shaft , tubing and casing can completely melt and drip and melt and drizzle and run and squirt and ooze and pulse and pulse and pulse and pulse....

(Pixie, completely overcome by lust cannot take it anymore.)

PIXIE: ENOUGH! I mean, 'How interesting'. I never knew there was so much...action....goin' on in one of them little things.

CHIP: Oh you'd be amazed ma'am by the size of the current in these tight little packages.

(Pixie is totally enraptured by the young man and lets out a guttural squeak.)

PIXIE: Young man...young....young....man.....would you care for some lemonade?

CHIP: Don't mind if do. If it's no bother.

(Chip continues to work while Pixie gets the lemonade.)

PIXIE: I don't recall seeing you around the penthouse before....uh?

CHIP: Oh. The names Chip! Chip Novemberino! My pop is the regular super for this building. I just got my associates degree in electrical engineering from San Pedro State and Pop needed some extra help for the summer! So here I am! I get to use my skill and bank 2 fifty an hour! What a lucky break, huh?

PIXIE: For all of us.

CHIP: Gosh, this is exiting! You could say that you are really breaking me in! I have very little practical experience. Oh sure, I've seen how all of the parts fit and work, but there's only so much satisfaction you can get from working on your own. Well, by golly! Here I am! Hard at work and totally willing to dive right in and get my hands dirty.

(Pixie crosses behind Chip and deliberately pours the lemonade on Chip.)

CHIP: Watch out!!

PIXIE: Oh, I am the clumsiest thing! I have completely soaked your work clothes!

CHIP: Jeez! Pop'll kill me!

PIXIE: Not to mention you being wet and near all those electrical currents. How dangerous!

CHIP: I just gotta finish this job. If I quit now, it would go against everything that an associates degree in electrical engineering from San Pedro State STANDS for!

PIXIE: I feel just awful!

CHIP: Gee if only I didn't have these wet clothes on.

(Pixies mouth contorts into an evil smile as her eyes narrow.)

PIXIE: I think I have a suggestion! Why don't you slip out of those wet things...I'll hang them here on the balcony. By the time you've finished with the wiring, your clothes will be dry and your Pop will be none the wiser!

CHIP: Say! That's a great idea!

PIXIE: I thought so...

CHIP: I hope you don't mind! I only got my skivvies on!

PIXIE: Are they wet too?

CHIP: Oh, I don't do that anymore….Oh gosh! You're talking about the LEMON-ADE!

PIXIE: Oh gosh yes!

(Chip peels out of his clothes. Soon, he is in his jockey shorts. He hands the clothes to pixie who is hyperventilating. Pixie takes the clothes out to the balcony.)

CHIP: Thanks, ma'am! Well, it looks like I am. Pretty dry otherwise. I'll go ahead and finish up. *(Chip kneels down to look at the socket.)* Saaaaay! We need to be extra careful. There's a pretty good wet spot here! We wouldn't want to step in this puddle while we're NEAR this electricity or KABOOM!

PIXIE: KABOOM!

CHIP: That's right!

PIXIE: Well, we'll just keep our eyes peeled.

CHIP: Gosh I'm so sticky right now!

PIXIE: That makes two of us…You know, I knew a young man just like you once.

(Out of no where, the ghostly vision of a young sailor dances into sight. He performs a tribute to Agnes DeMille ….one she never wanted. Pixie is in a reverie.)

PIXIE: He was a sailor, I was a girl of sixteen. Oh, I'll never forget him. Brick Lonigan. I wanted him the second I saw him. One night, I stole away and we met in secret on a nearby beach. I was willing to give myself to him, longing for his powerful touch and the red hot invasion of my passion. But something was wrong. The nearer I drew to him, the further he pushed me away. I ached for his caresses, but he would have none of it! He finally told me his—TERRIBLE—secret! Nature had played some cruel joke on my sailor boy. He could never love a woman. I was left unwanted and undesirable…

CHIP: Gee! You oughta send that one into Readers Digest! *(Chip stands.)*

PIXIE: You know what I'd like to do, young man? Young…young….young … young…man?

CHIP: No ma'am.

PIXIE: I'd like to kiss ya. Softly and sweetly on the mouth…

CHIP: Ma'am?

PIXIE: Look at me, Chip Novemberino.

CHIP: I'm looking ma'am.

PIXIE: Look at my supple flesh. My breasts heaving beneath my silken shift.

CHIP: I think I'm almost finished here, ma'am.

PIXIE: Why, we've not yet started young Chip. Touch me.

CHIP: What?

PIXIE: I said touch me!

(Pixie grabs Chips hands.)

CHIP: You're scarin' me ma'am!

PIXIE: Take my yielding flesh into your powerful hands and use me! Use me! Make me your Whore!!!

CHIP: Hey! Hey!

(Pixie grabs Chip around the neck and draws the lamp from the desk up to her face.)

PIXIE: Look at my face ,Chip. Have you ever seen such beauty? Don't you want me Chip? Or are you an invert like my little sailor man? Are you too afraid to know the touch of a woman?

CHIP: My toolbox!

PIXIE: I'LL GET TO THAT!!! Kiss me! TAKE ME!

CHIP: No! No! I'm saving myself for Grad School!

PIXIE: You can't reject me Chip! It's too powerful! The current between us! Our passion cannot be denied Chip! Will you ever be able to feel this spark with anyone else?????

CHIP: NOOOOOOO!!!!

(Pixie deliberately steps in the puddle of lemonade as she smashes a kiss into CHIPS mouth. Suddenly, real sparks begin to fly. And smoke! And fire. The sounds of electricity going crazy and the sizzle of burning flesh reverberates through the room. At once, the sights and sounds have concluded, and having been electrocuted by Pixie, Chip slumps dead to the sofa. Pixie switches off the lamp and wipes off the corners of her mouth.)

PIXIE: Looks like 15 years of electro-shock therapy paid off AFTER all!

(She suddenly realizes what she has done!)

PIXIE: Chip? Chip? No! Such beauty....I did it again! Everything I touch I destroy! I am evil! EVIL!

(Pixie slowly surveys the room with mounting panic.)

PIXIE: I'll go to Margot! She'll know what to do! Margot! Margot! Ya gotta help me! I'm in trouble!!!!!

(Pixie grabs the keys and runs into Margot's bedroom.)

(Silence.)

(Emory Enters with Miss Beezus. He is dressed in Kimono with a fluffy towel wrapped around his head. Under the robe, he is of course.....nude.)

EMORY: Miss Margot? I have the most devastating news! I was doing my Daily Crossword Puzzle and just GUESS who 27 down is! Miss Margot? Why is it so dark in here? I'll switch on the light!

(He does so.)

EMORY: Oh hello Viddy. I see your finally taking a little rest! Good for you! Ones health is SO important. Viddy. Viddy. Dear, I don't know how to tell you this but there appears to be a hammer

(Suddenly realizes she's dead.)

EMORY: STUCK INSIDE YOUR HEAD! OH DEAR GOD!

(He backs up across the room. Just then, Eddie's body tumbles from the closet.)

 EMORY: AAAAAAAAH! DEATH! DEATH EVERYWHERE!

(Starts to run and discovers Chip's half naked body on the sofa.)

EMORY: AAAAAAAAAH!

(Stops long enough to look down Chip's jockey shorts. Then suddenly...)

EMORY: BUTCHERY!! BUTCHERY!! DEATH AND BEAUTY! DEATH AND BEAUTY!

(Margot rolls in her chair. Se is disheveled. She has obviously been drugged.)

MARGOT: Who is it? Who is there? I can barely see....

EMORY: Margot! Dear Margot! Are you hurt?

MARGOT: Emory? Is it you? I thought I heard….screaming….

EMORY: Miss Margot, you have got to listen to me! That She-Beast sister of yours has finally gone completely and totally mad!

MARGOT: Really? What makes you say that?

EMORY: Oh, just one or two things lying around the apartment!

MARGOT: Who are all these people? Are we having a party?

EMORY: Margot darling, we have got to do something! Your insane sister has turned your classically appointed Sunset boulevard flat in to a CHARNEL HOUSE! Not all of the Canada Dry Soda in the WORLD is gonna get the BLOOD out of these Orientals! The time has come! Pixie has tasted gore, Margot! GORE! And she must be stopped before she KILLS AGAIN!

MARGOT: Kills …again…?

EMORY: We are going to call the hospital Margot. We are going to call Mayfair Regency Acres right now and have them come with an ambulance and a straight jacket!

(Emory picks up the phone and dials.)

MARGOT: Straight….jacket….

EMORY: Hello? Mayfair Regency Acres? Yes. There has been a murder….
MUUUUURRRRDER!!!!!

MARGOT: Wait Emory…..

EMORY: Just be calm Miss Margot! *(Back to the phone.)* What was that? Yes. I am in the home of Margot De Costa. 14th floor of the Hollywood Ritz Arms. Miss De Costas sister Pixie has run amok and has slaughtered half a dozen poor souls here today!

MARGOT: Emory, stop….

EMORY: I know what's best, Miss Margot! *(Back to the phone.)* We need ten of your strongest men to come and subdue this unholy beast...And make SURE they're ALL Latino!

MARGOT: Put...the...phone....down.....Emory.....

EMORY: Yes! Yes! Oh thank you, thank you!

(Margot suddenly stands up and removes her babushka, revealing herself to be 'PIXIE".)

PIXIE: Put the phone down Emory....

EMORY: Just a moment, Miss Margot! I have *(he sees her)*....I have....I have....I have....

('Pixie' takes the phone out of his hand.)

PIXIE: Gimme that thing, ya fruit! *(Speaks into the phone as MARGOT.)* I'm sorry. I'd like to cancel that order for ten strong Latinos and a straight jacket. Yes, I'm afraid my....nephew....was playing a little prank. *(Sweetly.)* Yes, he will be punished. Yes. Yes. Of course. Everything here is fine. Just fine. Mmmm hmm. Goodbye now.

EMORY: Where's Margot? What have you done with her?

PIXIE: What I shoulda done a LONG time ago. I KILLED HER! I finally poisoned that goody two shoes bitch! She's been a dead weight hanging around my neck for years. Jeez, she was too STUPID to DIE the FIRST time she hadda chance too. Who falls fourteen stories from a penthouse balcony and LIVES, for cryin' out loud!

EMORY: So it wasn't an accident! YOU PUSHED HER!!!!

PIXIE: YA DAMN RIGHT I PUSHED HER! She stole my work, she stole my fame, she stole my glory, SHE STOLE MY LIFE! SHE HAD TO BE STOPPED! And I finally did it! I'm free, I tell ya! Free! Never again will I have to put up with her lousy voice and her lousy manners and her lousy movies. I STOPPED HER! And now, I gotta stop you....

EMORY: No! No!

PIXIE: Yes! Yes! Come to Pixie and TAKE.... YOUR.....MEDICINE!!!!

(Pixie LURCHES at Emory. Emory tosses Miss Beezus into Pixies face!)

EMORY: Miss Beezus! Miss Beezus!

PIXIE: NOOOOOO! NOOOOO! MY EYES!!!! I HAVE NO INSURANCE!!!

(Miss Beezus howls to the heavens as she claws at Pixies eyes! Screaming, Pixie stumbles into the bedroom, Emory slams the door shut on her.)

EMORY: HELP! HELP! MURDER! MURDER!

(Emory races to the door just as officer O'Halleran Enters. Emory screams in terror!)

EMORY: AAAAAAAHHHH! Oh Detective! Thank God you arrived! Something AWFUL has happened!

O'HALLERAN: Detective Mike O'Halleran. What the Devil is going on here?

EMORY: Oh Detective! Thank God you arrived! Something AWFUL has happened!

O'HALLERAN: Oh REALLY? It wouldn't have anything to do with all these DEAD BODIES lyin' around would it?

EMORY: Why yes! That's uncanny!

O'HALLERAN: It's the training. Who's responsible for all this?

EMORY: She's *(sweeping dramatically to the door)* IN THERE!

(Calling for orderlies.)

O'HALLERAN: She's in here girls. In there. Make sure ya have plenty of tranquilizer with ya.

(The orderlies enter. One has a huge syringe. The other a straight jacket.)

ORDERLY: Don't worry, chief.

ORDERLY: Yeah. There is enough morphine in this syringe to bring down a water buffalo.

ORDERLY: Get a load of this place, will ya?

ORDERLY: Looks like all these broads taste was in there mouth.

EMORY: I'll have you know that these rooms were decorated by none other than Billy Haines!

ORDERLY: Yeah? And who did yer outfit? Anna May Wong?

(Emory is appalled. The orderlies exit into the bedroom.)

EMORY: *(Calling after them.)* Be careful in there....The bed curtains are chintz. Imported. *(Miffed.)* Philistines....

O'HALLERAN: Faith and Begorra. It's been years since I been up to the De Costa Penthouse.

EMORY: You've been here before?

O'HALLERAN: Them De Costa girls use to have me up to watch over things while they threw them wild parties. Yes, I was even here on the fateful night of ....the accident. Poor poor darlin' girl...

(Door opens and Pixie is led out by orderly.)

ORDERLY: Okay Chief. Here's your order—One over the hill nut-job to go.

ORDERLY: Ain't you ashamed?. What do you have to say for yourself?

PIXIE: *(Pixie has reverted to a child on Morphine.)* I am vewy vewy sawy I kilt all dees nice people.....

EMORY: Miss Beezus? Miss Beezus? Where's my darling Miss Beezus, you harridan?

PIXIE: I am vewy vewy sawy I kilt all dees nice people *(Pulls out the body of Miss Beezus—HEADLESS!)* and dis one big white cat.....

EMORY: Miss Beezus? NOOOOOOOOOO!

O'HALLERAN: Well, you go along with the good doctors here like a good girl.

PIXIE: Bye bye! Bye Bye!

(Pixie and the orderlies are gone.)

O'HALLERAN: Ah dear. She was so beautiful once.

EMORY: I'll never get over this as long as I live. Miss Beezus!!!! *(He wails.)*

O'HALLERAN: There there, little fella. Why don't ya go home and have the little lady cook ya a nice thick steak, toss back a beer and listen to the ball game on the radio.

EMORY: *(Confused.)* Is there someone else in the room? *(Suddenly.)* WAIT!

O'HALLERAN: What?

EMORY: MARGOT! Oh that dear, sweet woman. I suspected Pixie was insane all along! And now she has killed poor Margot

O'HALLERAN: What in the blue blazes are you goin' on about?

EMORY: Pixie confessed to me not two minutes before you got here! She practically cackled with GLEE while she went on about it! That Gorgon MURDERED MARGOT IN COLD BLOOD!

O'HALLERAN: You're nuts, Mac!

EMORY: It's true!

O'HALLERAN: I'm telling you it ain't possible!

EMORY: PIXIE DE COSTA CONFESSED IT ALL TO ME!

O'HALLERAN: *(Loudly and clearly.)* PIXIE DE COSTA FELL TO HER DEATH FROM THAT BALCONY TWENTY FIVE YEARS AGO!

EMORY: *(Stunned with terror.)* WHAAAAAAT?????

O'HALLERAN: Listen buddy, I don't know who you THINK you spoke with tonight, but Pixie De Costa is cold and dead and molderin' away out there in Forest Lawn!

EMORY: Nooooo!

O'HALLERAN: I remember it as if it were an hour and 35 minutes ago, plus intermission. The joint was jumpin' that night! Suddenly, I hear a scream and all hell breaks loose! Two movie producers drag me into the stairwell and have me usher Margot de Costa out the back door. When we get to the pavement, there was the mangled dead body of Pixie De Costa.... And there......and there....and some left over bits there....We scoop up Pixie, what was left of her anyway, and get rid of the evidence. Meanwhile, Margot gets sent to Palm Springs to cool her heels for a while.

EMORY: Its like something out of a Val Lewton movie, directed by Jacques Tournour and starring Simone Simon.....

O'HALLERAN: Unfortunately, there was a witness! A young girl reporter by the name of Helena La Mancha. She threatened to tell the world what she had just seen. Oh, she was Hot to make a name for herself, and blackmail was right up her alley. And them studio chiefs paid dearly. Helena gets herself a syndication and we get an alibi that sticks.

EMORY: How ugly…

O'HALLERAN: Only trouble is, down in Palm Springs, Margot ain't doin' too good. Seems she's started talkin' to herself. Only it AIN'T herself she's talkin' to. It's Pixie. And lord help us all when Pixie started talkin' back! The trauma split Margot De Costa in half so that her sister might live again. Too bad. The Worlds Greatest Star had become a liability to the studio. So them producers stick her up here under lock and key and watchful eye.

EMORY: Viddy?

O'HALLERAN: Yes. But even Viddy Johnson didn't have all the facts. All she knew was that Margot was delusional and she was here to protect her. And it looks like Viddy died tryin' to keep this story from getting to the wrong people. Like you, maybe? You seem like an awful chatty little feller.…

EMORY: N— n— n —n— n —n— n— no……

O'HALLERAN: *(Threateningly.)* Lets keep it that way….for your own good. Well, I best be off to see after Miss Margot. Or Miss Pixie. Whichever one she thinks she is now. Poor Darlin'…

(Helena enters breathlessly brandishing a camera.)

HELENA: O'Halleran! What the devil…?

O'HALLERAN: Ah, Miss La Mancha. I mighta known you'd get wind of this.

HELENA: You know me, Mike. I'd DIE to get the scoop on this story!!!

O'HALLERAN: Well, be careful what you wish for……HA HA HA HA HA HA!!!!!!!! *(He exits.)*

(Helena spies Emory and the bodies.)

EMORY: Margot….Pixie….Not Pixie….	**HELENA:** Say, what the hell…?
Only Margot…Miss BEEZUS!….	Pixie! Pixie!
Pixie Dead…..Margot….Not Dead…..	*(Finds Viddy.)*
Margot…..Margot….MARGOT!!!	Margot, MARGOT!!!

(Emory crumples to the floor, awash in emotion. Suddenly, his back straightens and he rises from the floor with all of the grace of a phoenix. Emory's dream has come true. He has become Margot De Costa.)

EMORY: Yes? Did I hear someone call my name? Oh no! I never get tired of signing autographs. You like my hair? I had it especially done for my new picture, 'Street Walking Saint!' I'll be playing opposite Robert Montgomery!

HELENA: Miss….De Costa?

 EMORY: Oh! The Press! I'm so glad you've come! Would you mind terribly if I freshened up a bit?

(He puts on Margot's Caftan.)

EMORY: I must prepare for a scene in my next film 'The Duchess and the Other Duchess'…You see I am saying goodbye to my darling Sebastian who is going back to the woman he loves, Rosamund…..My dearest, darling Sebastian. I do love you. With every breath I take, with every fiber of my being. But my heart Sebastian. My foolish, foolish heart. It knows I can never posses you…And so I must say….. adieu……

HELENA: We're ready for your close up Miss De Costa

(Emory, now completely Miss Margot, poses for posterity.)

(Helena flashes her camera.)

(She looks up in rapture and mouths a silent 'thank you' to an uncaring god...)

(Lights out.)

(Light comes up on Viddy. She crosses over to Chip.)

VIDDY: Yes lord. You're only as good as your last picture. For poor Mr. Emory, his last picture was the one in this morning's paper.

NEWSBOY: Good night nurse!

VIDDY: Wait a minute. Ain't you the Newsboy?

NEWSBOY: And the electrician. I told the producers the only way I would appear in my underwear was if they beefed up my part a little.

VIDDY: Honey, it looks like your part don't need any beefing up!

NEWSBOY: Aaaaaw....So what happened to Emory? And Margot?

VIDDY: Well, sugar, that Detective Mike O'Halleran fingered Mr. Emory for the multiple murders of Eddie Grant, Chip Novemberino, Miss Beezus the White Persian Cat, and *(looking at paper)* 'an unidentified maid'. Hmmph. I took a hammer to the head and they can't look in my pocket book to find my drivers license so they can get my damn name right? I am telling you. White people are nuthin' but hateful sometimes! 'Cept you, honey. We gonna get along fine!

NEWSBOY: Mr. Emory?

VIDDY: Mr. Emory ain't talkin'. You see he's off at the 'studio' in his mind getting' ready for Margot's next big picture. And Margot herself? Well, all them producers just weren't around anymore to protect her the way they use to. So she just sorta disappeared over night...this time for good. Which leaves this here place mighty empty. Or is it? Seems like there might just be a lotta ghosts clingin' to the wall paper of this old tomb. Ghosts that all know what really happened up here in the Penthouse on the 14th floor of the Hollywood Ritz Arms.

NEWSBOY: It's kinda sad isn't it?

VIDDY: Sad?

NEWSBOY: Everyone will forget us. I mean, even five years from now—who's gonna even care what happened to a paid companion, a hack screenwriter, a flamboyant bachelor, a Persian cat, a virginal electrician and two washed up movie stars?

VIDDY: Sugar, it is a tragic thing when any soul is forgotten. All any of us can do is hope…hope that someone will care enough to look back…to find the truth…the past…the faces…the names….the beauty that never fades….the stories that never end…the movies. And aren't we lucky to have them? They are the only magic that is left. Whenever you say Judy Garland, you remember and you are over the rainbow. Or if you say Ethel Waters, you remember, and happiness is a thing called Joe.

Say Lena Horn and you remember…

Say Hattie MacDaniel and you remember…

(The following lines are spoken by the cast in unison, ending at the same time.)

VIDDY:
Say Rex Ingram
Say Paul Robeson
Say Maidie Norman
Say Butterfly McQueen
Say Eddie Rochester Anderson
Say Dorothy Dandridge
Say Louise Beavers
Say Mantan Moreland
Say Claudia McNeil
Say Steppin Fetchitt
Say Bill Bojangles Robinson
Say Faynard Nicholas
Say Margot De Costa
Say Pixie De Costa
Say Pixie De Costa

EMORY:
Say Edward Everett Horton
Say Theda Bara
Say Gloria Swanson

NEWSBOY:
Say Jackie Cooper
Say Jackie Coogan
Say Mickey Rooney
Say Judy Garland
Say Lana Turner
Say Spanky McFarland
Say Alfalfa Schweitzer
Say John Wayne
Say Roy Rogers
Say Dale Evans
Say Tom Mix
Say Gene Autrey

HELENA:

Say Rudolph Valentino
Say Ramon Navarro
Say Carmen Miranda
Say Maria Montez
Say Steve Reeves
Say Robert Taylor
Say George Brent
Say Johnny Weissmuller
Say Pixie De Costa
Say Pixie De Costa
Say Pixie De Costa

O'HALLERAN:
Say Charlie Chaplin
Say Harold Lloyd
Say Buster Keaton
Say W.C. Fields
Say Mae West
Say Harpo Marx
Say Red Skelton
Say Bob Hope
Say Bing Crosby
Say Pixie De Costa
Say Pixie De Costa
Say Pixie De Costa

YOUNG PIXIE:
Say Shirley Temple
Say Jane Withers
Say Baby Peggy
Say Margaret O'Brien
Say Virginia Weidler
Say Pixie De Costa
Say Pixie De Costa
Say Pixie De Costa

Say Irene Dunne
Say Bette Davis
Say Jean Arthur
Say Alice Brady
Say Faye Bainter
Say Thelma Ritter
Say Barbara Stanwyck
Say Joan Crawford
Say Marlene Deitrich
Say Maureen O'hara
Say Pixie De Costa
Say Pixie De Costa
Say Pixie De Costa

EDDIE:
Say Erroll Flynn
Say Humphrey Bogart
Say Jimmy Cagney
Say Edward G. Robinson
Say Ray Milland
Say Bill Holden
Say Jimmy Stewart
Say Pixie De Costa
Say Pixie De Costa
Say Pixie De Costa

YOUNG MARGOT:
Say Eleanor Powell
Say Dick Powell
Say Ruby Keeler
Say Fred Astaire
Say Ginger Rogers
Say Pixie De Costa
Say Pixie De Costa
Say Pixie De Costa

VIDDY: Whatever happened to her?

THE END !!???!!?!

77

NOTES